Call an Angel!

Seventy-Two Angels and
their *Gifts* to Humanity

Call an Angel!

Angelic Self Help

*Healing, Growing
and Creating with the
Help of the Angels*

E. A. Terry

In Company with the Angels
Branson, MO

Library of Congress Cataloging-in-Publication Data

Terry, E. A, 1947-
     Call an Angel! Angelic Self Help. Healing, Growing, and Creating with the Help of the Angels / E. A. Terry. - 1st ed. Illustrations by E. A. Terry and P. E. Poe

        p. cm.
     ISBN 0-9649824-0-4

Cover by Wayne Slowik
Interior Design by E. A. Terry.
Illustrated by E. A. Terry and P. E. Poe.
Printed in the United States of America by C. J. Krehbiel.

Author's Note

Angels are vortices of energy. As they catch incoming higher frequencies and transmute these into lower frequencies that are more usable by humanity, they will begin to emanate with light frequency values that may be seen or sensed as colors by humans. These conscious beings of light catch and step down the incoming energies into very specific light and other energy values to meet the exact needs of humans traversing the path of life back to Oneness with, in, and of God.

This path of Oneness has a large emotional component and these angelic gifts of God are geared to meet this need with the exact counter balance of energies to bring fluid, graceful steps and completions. The seventy-two Angels represented in this glorious gift from God hold exact energies to heal and progress humanity far beyond these present growth steps.

This is where you choose. Are you ready for change, and do you consciously choose that now? I invite you to proceed with this volume *only* if this is your desire and choice now. These gifts of God through the Angels are explosively powerful in creating and changing. ***Proceed consciously.***

Allow your entire senses to embrace the depictions given by the Angels, to merge and blend energies for the shifts in equilibrium that they offer. Let their words resound through your being. Do remain open to further shifts and growth in your continuing cocreative status with the Angelic Realm. They will offer further energies of colors and Light and Love, swirling and flowing in growth and ascension. Open your mind, heart, and soul to these transformative gifts as you evolve in your own unique way, for the vast diversity of God's gifts to humanity can only be fully experienced by living it enthusiastically and joyfully.

No book will tell you how it will unfold and this one is only a suggested starting point, a jumping on point, for creations far beyond our joint capacity to envision now.

    Bon Voyage!!!

E. A. Terry

Acknowledgments

My warmest thanks to all of my friends for our growing, changing relationships, from which the Angels found fertile ground to experientially prompt me through this book. I especially want to thank John Prechtel for creating the initial space and place for me to choose to work with the Angels, Dawn Bothie for her supportive encouragement to talk with the Angels, and for the early channelings that pointed the way.

My thanks also to the different artists who patiently attempted to portray the Angels, only to finally have that joy fall to me! I especially thank Phyllis E. Poe for answering the Angels' and my call for help in completing the enclosed angelic portrayals. I thank Kathy Rawlings and repeat my thanks to Dawn Bothie for their loving and caring support through all my personal changes as I grew through the writing of this book with the Angels.

Special thanks to Beth and Lee, and to Mom and Dad for being there as I went through my ballistic growth. May God bless my persistent typesetter, Lara, for her choice to help me format this book. Warm thanks to Roger and Jim for answering my endless computer and business questions as I became more self sufficient in the publishing world.

I especially thank God and all of the seventy-two Angels in this book who stepped forward to answer humanity's call for help. Hopefully we will bless You in our use of these gifts, even as You bless us in the giving of these exquisite gifts.

CONTENTS

The Seventy-Two Angels and Their Gifts and Messages to Humanity

Contents

Contents

Indexes

Preface

The Angels are talking to humans now. What's different is that humans are starting to **hear** the Angels. With this turn of events, this change in our attention, seventy-two Angels have presented themselves for everyday assistance to humanity. Seventy-two have addressed humanity's greatest needs and desires and stepped forward to offer their hands as part of our team.

God never meant us to do this alone - '*this*' meaning living and growing, changing and evolving, loving and caring. Certainly we have families and friends, other people in embodiment alongside us, but it turns out we have lots of help in other realms, too--like the Angels. We have had this all along but we forgot, forgot to ask for help and allow it. We thought we had to do this alone, without any help from God. Well, thankfully, God's Messengers have arrived and are eager to help.

Just ask!! Call an Angel today and ask for help. This is a free will world and only by asking and allowing help do you get it. ***So ask today!!***

Introduction

by the

Seventy-Two Angels

Love and only love will soften the hearts and minds of humanity. All the logic that may be given will be as a token in a basket. The love of the mother for her child brings hope to a sufferer's heart and soul. A mother's love is ever hopeful, unconditional and expansive, always eager to share and love more. The Angelic Kingdom is a grand embodiment of maternal love, embracing all of humanity in its caring, nurturing wings. This is the gift we offer now. This and much more.

The masses of humanity are suffering heartache and, many of you, without hope. Your few pleasures barely keep you in your bodies to continue life. You have little hope for change and certainly few of you have any serviceable ideas of how to create uplifting change. Long have you, humanity, denied your union with God, All that Is, your true Inner Self! Long have you thought yourself beneath God, unworthy and unable to commune. Long have you created separation within and without.

No longer will this be tolerated or supported. It has been the Angels' quandary to connect with you, and in the past was possible only in moments of crisis, when your guard was down and a 'miracle' could be believed.

Now the Angels propose to present themselves, their energies for use on request to you, the mortal, normal male and female, for any of you who recognizes a need for a power greater than you believe you have. These angelic gifts to humanity are only to bring you awareness of the God within, to help you believe again, to know God again, and to revel in this knowingness and joy of Oneness. Until you open the door and enter the Godhead, the kingdom of God within, the Oneness with God, you are less than was meant to be.

The Angels are now given permission to reach out a hand to one who calls. This 'hand' will be mighty in the value that the caller asks for. If there is but a crack in your veils, your defenses, this Angel will enter and offer you assistance. If there is a pause, a moment of stillness, of belief, an openness, this Angel will begin to work their Angelic Magic. As more people ask for help, the Angels will be quicker and more powerful in answer to the call, always tempered to the caller.

Introduction

Know this. *WE,* the Angelic Realm, stand ready and eager to assist in all ways that are permitted. We do understand your sorrow, pain and confusion. We feel sorrow as we see humans continue in this plight unduly long. Hence our eager offer to help now. Know that it is our greatest desire to soften these sorrows and pains and lift these burdens from your shoulders. Together we can do this and much greater things.

God, All that Is, thrills at your steps of growth, your unfolding and your embrace of these truths, as you and we hold alignment in consciously recreating this Oneness.

We, the Angels, are here as tools to help humanity to awaken to the God within, the Oneness expressing through you. As part of God's team and humanity's team simultaneously, we offer our assistance to open awareness, to bolster belief that 'you can do it,' you can change!

Just ASK!! Just ask and allow that these changes are possible and even probable now. We are here and eager to help. Stir yourselves from the lethargy of unbelief. It is a thing of the past. Now all is possible, so believe and choose carefully, consciously. Go for the stars! Join us. We await your call.

Segment One

The How To's of Calling Your Angel

When you invite the Angelic help of the seventy-two Angels, the appropriate Angel(s) *will* step forward. These Angels are on 'go' and just waiting for your invitation to begin cocreating with you, amplifying your energies, and facilitating your manifestations to fulfill your desires and needs. This tool allows you to participate consciously and overtly, with deliberate intent and openness to this assistance.

They, the Angels, hear your call, your silent cry anywhere and anytime, with an immediate response. Yet they move in reverence and grace.

Your Higher Self will work in tandem with the Angels for quickest results. A good practice is to ask for Higher Self communication, and obtain an open line to *your* Higher Self ("my Higher Self of this body, consciousness, time line and location") first, then ask for the Angel or Angels that can best help you with the situation at hand now to step forward.

Several methods of allowing this Angel to come forward will work. You can just *open the book randomly* and allow the most prominently effective Angel to jump out to you. If you feel compelled to repeat this, the Angels are probably prompting you to allow another to come forward. So *repeat as you feel to*, with your question or situation needing attention in mind.

If you keep a journal, you can ask and allow the Angel(s) that you need for help at the time of journaling to come into your awareness, and speak directly to you via your journaling. When you open your awareness and request that the Angels help you, they may well come to you directly, by appearing to you, speaking to you, or coming in through your journaling. The Angels only have the opportunities that you create for them.

When your Angel(s) have come forward in whatever way they come into your awareness, then allow your hand to *touch and feel the colors* of the Angelic portrait. When portrayals are unavailable, allow your own reception of the colors of the summoned Angel. Call the Angel's name three times in reverence and expectancy. See the vibrant shifting tones and feel the Angel's energies begin their work with you. Simply run your fingers and awareness over the curves of the Angel's wings in the

7

portrait and breathe in the colors represented there and in the rest of the picture to feel the Angel called and join energies with this Angel of choice. *Express your desire* for help and allow for an outcome that may be well beyond the scope of your imagination.

Each Angel picture holds the energy of the Angel portrayed. This energy is in a concentrated form and as you, the requester, touch and trace the curves of the wings, the color swirls, you merge energy with the Angel and you *then become One with the Angel*, with the increased insight and awareness of how to 'heal' the situation, how to energize the situation for an exquisite outcome.

You will feel this through yourself. This wisdom, these feelings, and this energy feel like (and *are*) your own energies amplified by the Angel's added energy. This brings remembrance of how to create, and forms the basis for you, the individual, to be independent of additional help. This also brings remembrance and opening awareness of our constant link to God, for Angels live in Oneness with God, and they amplify His energies within the human body and awareness.

This is the gift of the Angels, that they are ready and waiting for your call. Only your attention, your desire, and your expectancy are needed as you focus on the angelic portrait or message of your chosen Angel, calling in the Angel and unifying with this messenger of God. Use this technique with reverence and gratitude for best results. So simple. Just call. *Call an Angel!*

You may want to journal your desires and requests as well as outcomes, as the changes will transform your life in magical ways and often at a ballistic rate. This will help you solidify your requests within your heart and mind as you formulate and write specific and detailed wishes. Knowing and acknowledging your desire is the first step in creating it.

If you don't know what you want, but you know you need change, state that and *ask for help* in changing your situation and knowing what change and what direction would be best for you now. The alphabetical listings of the Angels and their gifts will also help guide you, and offer some qualities and outcomes that you may find desirable. Feel which qualities are preferable, which processes you would like assistance with, just what you are drawn to, and go with that feeling.

In summary:

1. *Acknowledge* that your have a *team* available, and *invite* the teamwork with the Angels and God.

2. *Recognize a need or desire* for change now.

3. Assess your ability to affect this change now, and *invite the assistance of the Angel(s)*, without a predefined outcome, for a most creative result.

4. To *select the Angel(s)* that can assist with the desired results, *call on your Higher Self to assist* and direct this. Determine that you actually have your Higher Self by stating that you want 'your Higher Self of this body, consciousness, time line and location.' Get a 'yes' to this, then proceed.

5. Use a *random method to select* the Angel(s), like opening the book randomly. This will allow for the participation of the Higher Self.

6. *To connect* with the Angel(s) called, *look* at the portrait, and *touch* the colors, *tracing* the curves with your fingers. If no picture is available, ask and allow the Angel's energies to come to you directly. *Call the Angel three times* in reverence and expectancy.

7. *Ask for the assistance of the Angel(s)*, and listen for the answer. Don't hang up! You may actually begin to get your answer immediately.

8. *Thank the Angel(s)* as if your request has already been filled.

The portrayals of the Angelic ones will nudge you as the viewer into the desire and willingness to 'have more of that' within yourself, thereby opening the door and creating the beginnings of an invitation to embody the portrayed angelic energies. It is a desire within you, the viewer, to experience more of this particular angelic energy. Initially you may feel as if this angelic energy enters from outside of yourself. With continued desire and repetition, this may feel, and indeed is, the angelic oneness awareness awakening within you, the caller and viewer. The summoned Angel will answer within the awareness of you, the caller, as part of your awareness.

This is a beginning glimpse of the emerging unity with all of creation. Stronger, fuller merging can be invited and allowed for grander experiences of Oneness.

These steps toward unity will certainly give rise to a myriad of experiences related to controlling behaviors and fears of losing individually, as this inevitable paradigm shift begins to occur with ever increasing rapidity.

The actual reality is Oneness, though humans have created the experience of separateness as an enrichment exercise on Earth. To open to re-merging within this density is the overall goal of this experience, bringing more subtleties of Light variation to the creation of each moment, as you shift from duality to Oneness.

Angels on Your Team

Life with Angels becomes higher dimensional very quickly. Inner awareness connected with outer awareness is the norm with the Angels everywhere--inner and outer. The creational possibilities with the Angels at your side expand exponentially. You become purposefully intentional as you discover your team and allow them to carry the ball some of the time.

And the rules change! Many things become possible and probable when you begin to acknowledge our Angelic friends and consciously work with them.

What would life be like if you were tapped into your inner knowingness, with your intuition fully active? Have a question and immediately have the answer. What would work be like if competition became cooperation? A lot more productive and fun, that's what!

Want to be able to understand what animals, plants, and crystals have to say? Call on Liriel, the Angel of Music to help open your pathways of hearing to the original intent and actually be able to converse with pets, plants, and even the Earth!

The possibilities are open ended as you begin to work and play with the Angels. Humans have some responsibility to participate here, and the higher frequencies bathing the Earth now will prompt you to change, will open your heart to belief in possibilities of changes far greater than have been possible in Earth's histories.

As men and women call on Angels, they *will* answer. They stand ready. An entire mosaic of possibilities is emerging that is grand, indeed, in effect and in beauty. The Angelic gifts are powerful in boosting humanity out of inertia and blindness, out of ignorance of your (and all humanity's) own true nature and abilities.

These seventy-two Angels, as you work and play with them, have the capacity to change the course of history, the essence of Earth, shifting all of humanity into a totally new awareness.

Ask for help from the Angels and *know* that, up front, you *will* move to be in your Truth. To open to the Angels is the first step to Truth. If you are holding any patterns that are not aligned to you, these will begin shifting. You will bring up values, belief systems, and principles to examine for validity in your life. You will begin to sift through your entire life to heal areas previously closed off from love.

Allow this angelic assistance. Open to feeling again, and owning your feelings, being who you are now, letting go of past impressions that scarred you and have since directed your life from those dark recesses of hurt. As these old feelings come up, feel them, accepting the child within who did all you knew to do, did the very best you could. Bless the child and let go of the feelings, allow them to soften and love this child, *you*, for the great effort, for doing all you could. Bless all others who participated, helping with this opportunity. *Feel.* Repeat until easy and complete.

You and many others--you are not alone here--have lived entire lives being ruled and directed by this hurt child within, emotionally frozen at the time of emotional trauma, continually repeating scenarios to try to resolve the pain. In this space you are unwittingly living life in the past, losing touch with the 'why' of your feelings, only knowing that is how it is for you.

Open to the assistance of the Angels, the help to open the closed doors of your pain and sorrow, your anger and sadness, all of your hurt. Allow the gentle, loving embrace of the Angels to protectively soothe your beingness as you re-experience the past hurts and fears, allowing the bursting of the intense feelings and subsequent dissipation in your release of the experience. Allow the assistance of the Angelic Realm to drain the boil of old emotions, to flood the infected area with their pure angelic essences to bring balanced and aligned life back into you.

This may mean allowing some quiet introspective time to write your autobiography. Allow your attention to start as early as you can remember. Write the enjoyable and the less enjoyable. Allow time at the less enjoyable sections to feel and heal with the Angels.

You will find where you, with the help of others, inserted and started running programs that are still active and running, but which are no longer your truth. The keys to changing these programs are the release and transmuting of the great emotional load holding them, these old tapes, in place and running.

Once this is processed, be sure to rewrite the tape in your truth, and put that to running in your systems, in your mind, heart and body. Always immediately fill the created void with your truth. Nature abhors a vacuum, so choose consciously what you want and pop that in.

More on the Process

Numbing out, abstaining from feeling or participating is a choice to abstain from life. Your opportunities in life are meant to be lived completely, to gather and complete the lessons woven into these scenarios. To abstain is to delay lessons, which will return with greater force each time until you embrace the lesson. You will orchestrate crisis upon mounting crisis until you cannot ignore the lesson any longer, and perforce if necessary, you embrace it, live it, and emerge all the wiser and richer for the results garnered.

Many of you on Earth are opening to your inner healing and examining the fibers of your life. Often the first impulse is to throw everything out and change your life *now*. Or you look to start throwing parts out, for a chance at a fresh start.

The fresh start happens in earnest when you look inside and take responsibility for yourself first. Looking outside of yourself for causes is to deny yourself as creator, and to deny that you are responsible for how you feel. There are no rights or wrongs in your life, just choices. Your choices have gotten you where you are, so keep choosing, but do choose differently to get different results.

We, the Angels, as you, are pure energy. Angelic energy is light without the density and lower frequencies that you as humans are living, and yet we are all energy. Keep the energy moving to keep life lively.

We dare to say happiness is a product of life lived fully rather than the purpose of it. Happiness has many flavors and all result from flowing your energies fully, living your opportunities.

When you are ready for a change in life, no need to discard all you have done, or wait for an opportune time. Just start in the moment to choose to feel again. Look inside, and know you are who and what you are by choice, and *you* and only you can change that.

Open to old scars, old hurts as a starting place to feel again, for these likely are where you stopped feeling, and possibly started blaming, hoping someone else was responsible for your pain. Open and feel, breathe and move, cry and laugh. Writing out these memories will help you remember more, and give you pause to feel again. Processing these old emotions back to positive feelings will help you restart your feelings again.

Allow the internal support system of the Angelic Realm and your Higher Self *and* have an external support system in place to assist as well for balance, as you begin to move and reintegrate into life again.

Honor others in their choices and scenarios. Do not usurp their lessons, or short circuit their learning opportunities to protect them or save them from pain. Just as parents and teachers must allow effect to follow cause with children, so do all of you need to act and get results, realizing the effects of your choices.

Compassion is great love and understanding, but it is rarely rescuing another or doing it for them. Compassion would be more of allowing one to continue a lesson and appreciating them regardless of their present scenario. Compassion has a very light touch, but is effective, nonetheless, in conveying self worth and self value,.

Your physical, mental, emotional, and spiritual bodies are living prisms with energy centers, chakras, that accept, spin, and flow the different colors and qualities of light. Your life is a dance through these energy colors, learning how to flow the colors and reintegrate them through the human body, aligning and reintegrating the energies, pushing out the blocks to this light, as you become less dense and more just pure light energy.

Live life with enthusiastic feeling. Accept help internally and externally from your teams. The Angelic Realm is ready and eager to assist all who choose life and asks for this assistance. This is a *self help manual*. The Angels can help you do it better, but 'do it' you must, since you are the being in the 3D body, attempting to transmute it to higher frequencies. This is the blue print of how to join in life again and live it far more fully than you can possibly know. Join us - The Angelic Realm!

Humanity's History of Change

Let it be known that the emotions of fear, pain, and hurt draw the Angels strongly to people with these experiences, as they are most in need. These emotions frequently immobilize individuals physically, emotionally, mentally, and spiritually. These people are *most* in need.

Fear immobilizes, freezes individuals or diverts their intentions into long side roads of adventure. This kind of adventure has become tiresome for many and they are ready to exit their treadmill of existence or change their life story now.

The opposite of fear is love, and in this case, the willingness to experience the choices you make, to embrace the totality of your choices. It is the willingness to go deep within and be who you are in the moment, to feel the spark of God within.

Each of you comes to Earth, knowing forgetfulness will overtake all (or most) of you and that you will at some point re-emerge from this forgetfulness and remember that you are here as portions of God to experience His creation, this being your gift back to the Creator.

In embracing every creation, every opportunity that you create, you *fall into alignment* with the original game plan of humanity on Earth. *In feeling, fully experiencing life, in truth, making conscious choices, you move from the immobilizing fear into the free flow of cocreation and love with your Creator.* This movement is key, essential to forward movement and eventual ascension from third density.

Creational Probabilities

Balance shimmers and ripples as you emerge, tenaciously trying life, breathing through long closed areas of being, reaching new equilibriums in each moment. Feeling and tasting of these reclaimed portions of self, you hold on a plateau momentarily to enjoy life around you, opening and questing for further steps of expansive life.

Risk taking, allowing new balances to ripple through life, creates opportunities for unscheduled random growth and expansion in life. Allowing celestial variables to interplay in life creates even more surprising and incredible results on a myriad of planes, these interconnecting and influencing one another for an explosive yet intentional chaos of growth.

With risk taking, not knowing or even attempting to direct the outcome, growth umbrellas into an effluence of expansive progression that can flower and blossom in free flowing abandon to create a scene far beyond what your sketchy desires would envision.

Tapping into your greater self, your forgotten and previously rejected parts of the soul, pulling in and reintegrating your parallel lives expands your possibilities and choices in life exponentially, far beyond your simple intellectual beliefs.

Opening to the higher dimensional parts of your selves and your teams creates further quantum possibilities, as life and beingness expand inwardly and outwardly simultaneously.

Needless to say, you may want to attend your physical body and its smooth, energetic functioning to be agile, graceful, and quick enough for living life through these new pathways of Love and Light. Will your emotional body of experiences and feelings allow you to risk these new pathways of growth in expansive abandon and joyous flow?

Can you allow yourself the freedom to grow and change, to trust and care, to create and be a part of your creation, to be fully 100% present? Can you release yourself from your intellectual restraints to soar and glide in the freedom of change, creational shifts and tilts, creative limbos between sweet culminations and new beginnings?

Do you dare to grow? To admit that stagnation is yielding little comfort and less satisfaction in your life? Do you dare to move from the crumbling security of *status quo* into a completely new dimension of living?

New Earth is a new reality, never before created or even envisioned, a new *create-as-you-go* endeavor with humans as the emerging race to star in the show.

The only way to negotiate the pathways of life now in this emerging society is to be completely present, attentive in the moment, recreating your choice of reality as you go. Everything is possible, as your desires, intentions, and thoughts create your world around you.

Choose well, dear friends, as you breathe in the fresh air of your fragrant new world. You are the creators of this creation with vast possibilities and infinite choices. Choose well and consciously for all is One, and so each choice impacts self and everything else.

The Angelic Realm is part of your reality now as energetic facilitators to boost and invigorate your choices. Invite this help if you choose. Allow the team play of your realm to overlap and intertwine with the celestial realms for miraculous splendor with mind and heart expanding results.

With these ever expanding experiences, awareness continues to iris open to broader and more encompassing knowingness. You come to know you are in every thing, and God is in you, and all comes into Oneness. Your resolved focus of unity with all of creation, with Oneness in God yields an infinite peace, which rolls over into infinite understanding, compassion, appreciation, and caring.

You look on your creations and care. You imbibe hope and connectedness in all you look upon and mold into further creations. You create in your own truth, with sincere appreciation of the wonder of all of creation including others' truth, others unique contributions to New Earth.

Secure and happy in your own creations of life, with effulgent joy, you openly appreciate the beauty of the subtle to flagrant diversity of others. This explosive display of enjoyment is fully accepted and reciprocated in joyful abandon, a nurturing scenario if there ever was one!

The choice is yours. Join in this New World creation if you dare to ascend, to accept these gifts of God and join the ranks of acknowledged, responsible and joy filled creators.

The Angels are God's messengers to help you know yourself. To help you know that you are a creator, and that all you need is inside of yourself *now*. The Angels will help activate your latent abilities and expand them into serviceable tools, accurate and dependable, strong and yet gentle, knowingness with compassion, all under your own intention, with the guidance of your Higher Self

Know that all of this is at your beck and call, but call you must! None will infringe upon your free will, not even your Higher Self, so you must request assistance and then direct it.

The Angels (and God) await your call. ✿

The
72 Angels

&

Their Gifts
and Messages
to Humanity

Segment Two

The Twenty Angels

Angel of Change, Anrijoyelle
Angel of Truth, Enuliel
Angel of Resolution, Hikalea
Angel of Synchronicity, Clelenael
Angel of Perfection, Alijana
Angel of Faith, Erehdenael
Angel of Forgiveness, Akenisael
Angel of Desire, Omlipon
Angel of Thinking, Jehmorael
Angel of Divine Will, Sekoisie
Angel of Ascension, Astonae
Angel of Comfort, Lihjolei
Angel of Life, Holmisei
Angel of Brotherhood, Peikule
Angel of Simplicity, Muriel
Angel of Cooperation, Hilojael
Angel of Unity, Miru
Angel of Diversity, Jarael
Angel of Intuition, Kenije
Angel of Emergence, Mohee

Anrijoyelle

Angel of Change

I am the Angel of Change and I offer you assistance in the power of flow, of movement and change. I nudge you forward and energize your transitions. I lovingly caress your choice to move forward in life. I can lighten your load with my powerful arms, assisting with my loving embrace. I touch your cheek lovingly to remind you of my joyful presence when you accept my assistance. I am joyful and graceful and yet I move with the power of the wind. Let me uplift you now in joy and peace and love, in clarity of your chosen direction. I am Anrijoyelle (pronounced *ahn ree joy el*).

When you are unhappy, feeling stuck, feeling that life is an endless treadmill, you know it is time for change, but how? Unclear on direction, unsure of strength, call me, your Angel of Change, for energy to know what direction, and strength to begin the move. Change yourself and your whole reality changes. Since you only have control over yourself, that is a good place to start. I stand ready to lift your heart and eyes in appreciation of change, in celebration of completions and beginnings.

When you have sunk to the lowest position in life, to the deepest feelings of hopelessness, call me. I am eager to assist in your change, and these heavy, disharmonic feelings are only the flags that reveal your absolute need for change. I stand ready to lift you and ease your movement, to create miraculously enjoyable

Anrijoyelle.
Angel B
change

change, as you release the old and create the new. Open your mind to the new insights that flood in, the warm energy of strength to move, and the eager insistence, that it is indeed *time* for change.

Touch the violets, lavender, pinks, light blue, the yellows in my portrait. Trace the curves of the wings, the very colors reflecting change and ascension of your energies. With reverence and expectation, in joy and love, receive.

I am at your side, your helper in change, ever eager to lend assistance. I bring joy to every step you make that is in a proper, uplifting direction. Choose change and I will open your heart to believe, your mind to know, and your soul to be the new person you choose to be.

Open your arms to my gentle nudges to change your life, to feel my embrace supporting you when you would fall, to know the joy and satisfaction of change from within. I am your Angel of Joyful Change, Anrijoyelle, here to assist you in life changing experiences. ✿

Enuliel

Angel of Truth

et it be known those of you with fear, pain, and hurt draw the Angels strongly as you are *most* in need. Fear frequently immobilizes you physically, emotionally, mentally, and spiritually, freezing your movement or diverting your intentions into long side roads of adventure. The tiresomeness of this kind of life has many of you ready to exit your treadmill of existence or change your life now.

The opposite of this immobilizing fear is willingness to experience the choices you make, to embrace the totality of your choices. The willingness to go deep within and be who you are in the moment, to feel the spark of God within. Truth literally can set you free of fear and this is your opportunity to embrace your own truth and live it.

I am Enuliel (*in new lee el*), your Angel of Truth. I can help you take an in-depth look at the truth of your life, knowing that you have created what you have and are now, by choice. Your choices may not always be in total alignment with your highest 'good', but progress toward your ultimate, or not so ultimate, goal is made one step at a time. So even 'missteps' are appropriate, to create the opportunity to make more supportive steps.

I come forth to assist in your creation, through your belief systems, for as you believe, so is your truth. I am Enuliel, your Angel of Truth, here to assist you in combating fear, in living truth. I strengthen the patterns of creation, and hold the energies of flow, of movement through these patterns.

Call me, your Angel of Truth, when you are ready for truth, whether that be deep in your heart or blatant before your eyes. Often you refuse truth and work at cross purposes to your chosen goals. *Allow your fear to dissolve as I embrace you in the Light of your truth, and assist you on your journey home.* My power is immense to create the freedom of movement you so desire.

Take time to deliberate your choices and feel the results of this. Be aware of this choice, whatever it is, being your own choice and not another's. Feel the truth of your choice, take a step, make another choice,and move forward in your chosen direction. Choose to be conscious and act consciously, in alignment with your own truth.

Humanity, in embracing every opportunity that you create, *falls into alignment* with the original game plan for humanity on Earth. *In feeling and fully experiencing life in truth, making conscious choices, you move from the immobilizing fear into the free flow of cocreation and Love with our Creator.* This is essential to forward movement and eventual ascension from third density.

Being true to yourselves, accepting your own truth above others' offerings, brings you into alignment with all of creation. The power of this alignment propels you forward at great speed. As you choose one thing and embrace it, fully experience this choice, then release this desire and grow on to another choice, and another. The process now is to feel and shift, feel and make another decision, one step at a time.

Movement is key. Truth allows movement physically, mentally, emotionally, and spiritually, through and between these four bodies. Breathe in your truth and embrace it. Feel my wings of Truth lift you in your chosen direction.

I shine with the Light of Truth and urge you to *move* in your truth. Breathe fully of your own truth, allowing yourself the fullness of time to make conscious choices and feel the results. Take a step toward your truth, with my hand to uplift you. Feel. Step again. Feel and step and you are on your way in truth.

My Light dissolves the fear that immobilizes and turns you from your truth. Call me. I am ever present and ready to assist and hold Truth in Light. Call on me always for a life of free flowing joy in truth. I am at your service. *I am Enuliel.* ✿

Enulich
Angel of
Truth

Hikalea

Angel of Resolution

Resolution happens within first, with letting go of fear, by embracing and dancing with your shadow, by allowing yourself to peek inside and see, feel, and know your true self, complete with the rejected fragments from earlier hurtful experiences.

Life often hurts. It's a trial of love guiding you blind and deaf, dissociated from yourself within, in duality, living the polarities, with the wish and hope for resolution of the opposites and return to Oneness.

Resolution begins with honoring yourself and others for who you are and where you are on the evolutionary ladder, 'you' meaning they as well. Allow yourself choices, your *own* choices, without competing. Allow others their choices, as the best for them, by their own choosing. Many are operating at different frequencies, so vision and abilities or lack of them are by circumstance, for a reason, and by personal choices.

You have orchestrated life, choosing scenarios to learn, to connect and open awareness between the segmented portions of self. It is hard living life without awareness, blind and deaf to the cries of the self, wondering if anyone is out there, does anyone hear you? You orchestrate scenarios to create resolution, crises after crises that force you toward change and resolutions. These fragmented parts of yourself, through challenging and enlightening experiences, get glimpses of each other and begin to hear the messages over the cries.

Hikalea,
Angel of
Resolution

E.A. Terry 9/66

and objections of the ego. The dissociation within the human structure has created grand ego opportunities. The ego will put on a fine dance to keep you from the awareness of Oneness, to continue to hold sway in your consciousness and your life.

Over time you often pack armor around yourself, layer upon layer, to insulate you from life, to keep you from feeling, moving, and interacting beyond your believed capacity or choice.

Your life is your mirror of yourself. Trying to fix reflections, fix everything outside of yourself, creates little change within or in the situation in front of you. Look to yourself. This is where you can affect change and eventual resolution. Heal, change within, embrace the lesson, grow and the mirror changes its reflection because you have changed from within.

Blame is refusing responsibility for your life reality. Resolutions won't hold, are elusive as long as blaming is your choice, blaming anything or anyone outside yourself for your reality.

With more and more experience, you evolve and the crises become less necessary as integration proceeds and your separate parts open to allowing and accepting one another, proceeding into open communication, and eventual wholeness.

Reintegration is now occurring on Earth, and humanity is choosing to remove the armor, layer by layer and feel life, breathe in life experiences again. In addition to the allowing, with more understanding of the process of life and risk taking, going for the gold in your aura, you are also holding your resonance and connection to God, rather than interacting at and descending to the lowest frequency levels of your life interactions.

When you hold your resonance in a situation, hold to your truth and identity, you are a gift to all others in the interaction, for you show them how to stand in their truth and be themselves as well.

These are steps of resolution, steps toward peace within, steps toward embracing life, looking for the lesson, taking responsibility for the creation of your own reality. Resolution is not so much a goal as a way of living peacefully in joyful creation. Life is in equilibrium. It is a system that will always move to maintain equilibrium, so changes within *will* affect, cause changes in, your relationships and situations.

If you choose to accept responsibility, this will mean embracing yourself, complete with all of your shadows, the less desirable parts of your self, and coming to terms with these. Allow these shadows to come forward in your awareness now. I, Hikalea (*high kay lee ah*), the Angel of Resolution, will assist you in strength and resolve to see and feel these parts of yourself with greater understanding and acceptance, greater appreciation for the struggle of the child within who so wanted to succeed, to do it right, to maintain the God connection. Know that you never lost your connection to God, ever, although you often felt and believed you did, so heavy and thick was the armor. Know that you are forgiven, for there is nothing to forgive, except that you forgive yourself.

Embrace all parts of yourself in allowance, acceptance and appreciation for having done and been all that you knew to be at the time. Breathe in Divine Love and Light, the elements needed to heal and fill the shadows with Light. Open to the Divine Love of God in the full appreciation of *all* aspects of you. These shadow aspects and qualities take on new light and value in the Light of Divine Love. Open to the acceptance and appreciation, and feel the resolution inside. Forgive yourself, thereby defusing the emotional triggers and transmuting the strong emotions that you held away from yourself as hurtful into loving acceptance. Breathe fully of the life force flowing through you and radiating from you. Let go of the fear, and open to the grand healing energy of loving acceptance.

This is the process of uniting the polarities, balancing the internal male and female energies into a merged alliance. Moments of choosing and creating peaceful resolution within are pivotal points in life, in choosing a new paradigm of living in grace. Humanity, in choosing reintegration within your individual selves, the whole of humanity, *and* your whole ecosystem, is in the process of a monumental paradigm shift. These moments of resolution form the creative platform for humanity to be the creative intendors of a grand future in peace, love and joy, abundance and ease.

We are of One breath, all of us. Choose to live in Love, appreciative and grateful for your lessons and opportunities. By choosing to accept responsibility for your personal reality and your ecosystem as a whole, your intent and awareness breathes life force into all of it. You become more conscious of your effect on yourself and your reality, and how *it is you*. Intention directs thought. Thought creates.

I am Hikalea, your Angel of Resolution, and I offer infinite attention on resolutions in life, toward alternative options, and movement in changing realities. Invite and allow my assistance for smoother, faster resolutions in greater alignment with Divine Truth. Open to the possibilities of miraculous outcomes beyond your personal conception. Miracles are probable now with you opening to your own creatorship, taking responsibility for your reality. Your creator abilities will blossom with this awareness. All of humanity can begin to create miracles.

Call me, Hikalea, when you are ready to create these miraculous resolutions. I stand ready to assist, your Angel of Resolution. ✿

Clelenael

Angel of Synchronicity

I am your Angel of Synchronicity, perfect timing for the perfect orchestration of events and happenings. This timing aspect is a weaving of energies for beginnings and endings and everything in between in life to happen with perfect timing, smooth flow, and the desired outcomes. Many energies in addition to time are woven into the fabric of your existence, all being necessary for the desired outcomes.

Many of you long for certain happenings and changes in your life. Know that these will occur in good time, in fact at the most perfect time, when you are completely ready, and not before or later. Timing is important for your comfort and for the effective results you so desire.

God has not forgotten you. You are in God's heart and awareness at all times. Only as you release and change, learn and grow in readiness, can more be revealed to you. Your veils are your chosen insulation, protection, and limitation. No steps are skipped. All in good time.

Timing at this particular time in Earth's history is changing. Time is moving, shifting, folding, compressing, and expanding. It is unpredictable now as never before, as Earth and all of her inhabitants shift into higher frequencies in change and transition, in the process of ascension.

Clelenael
Angel of
Synchronicity

I am Clelenael (*cluh len ay el'*), and I offer my assistance and guidance now for you to know right timing. Be still and listen. Listen inside and you will know more of this timing and the value of the events you orchestrate in your life, be they stillness, gentle growth steps or explosive eruptions. I am your Angel of Synchronicity, holding the balance for perfect timing of all events in your life. Before embodiment you decided what you would accomplish and do in this lifetime, so you are on a pre-determined course, and your choices along the way adjust the timing.

I offer now to share this knowledge of timing with you, so that as you know, understand, and accept this aspect of the orchestration of all in your universe, that you and I can work smoothly together for the desired outcomes.

While in school house Earth, some of you may continue to have anchors and veils restricting movement and vision. You move within boundaries on this plane and gradually evolve, with the veils and anchors thinning and changing as you grow more aware.

I offer my assistance to help keep you *in sync*, so that you are present and ready as forces coalesce to assist you in life's creation. You have all experienced being at the right place at the right time. You've all felt how smooth and easy some days go, how everything happens just right. You were *in sync*. I offer my help to make this your experience all of the time.

Invite my energies to help you be in sync consistently. My energies are smoothing and calming, yet energetic and enthusiastic. This gift of synchronicity will facilitate your growing awareness of how to time your creations and events in your life for the most effective outcomes. This balancing energy I offer as a daily experience. It's simple. Just call, and I'm there in no time at all! ✿

Listen inside and you will know more of this timing and the value of the events you orchestrate in your life, be they stillness, gentle growth steps, or explosive eruptions . . .

~Angel Clelenael

Alijana

Angel of Perfection

 am Alijana (*ah ley jah nah'*), God's Angelic Messenger, and I come forth to gift humanity with the essence of *perfection*.

Your perception of perfection on Earth is that it is largely unattainable in the forms that you desire and strive to create. This perception is especially true for those of you that have a faint memory of perfections of other realms. Yet God sees all as perfect in the moment, so your definition of perfection may shift with acceptance of perfection at each step of the process.

Perfection is not a goal so much as degrees of creations, layers of creation as you mold and shape your reality. Your reality, *your creations* will 'shape shift' before your eyes as you grow and change within.

My gifts of perfection are multifold, indeed, for the gifts of God that I deliver have layers of perfection to the energies. While every step you take is 'perfect' in God's eyes, we as cocreators can choose and appreciate certain balances, alignment, colors, and designs for the overall effects of these in the big (or little) picture. Enter *free will*. Even your learning processes are perfect as your unfolding awareness creates myriad scenarios.

I invite you to call on my partnership to see, feel, and be perfection in the moment, to appreciate your flawless unfoldment of awareness, and to spur that growth on to greater expressions of perfection. My boost of the essence of perfection will bring you clearer awareness of the perfection of your life and the vast possibilities before you. I, Alijana, await your call. ✿

Alijana
Angel of Perfection

Erehdenael

Angel of Faith

I, Erehdenael *(er den ay el),* come forth now to fill your cup, to assure your faith, your connection to God and that inner Being of you that is God. Faith *is* that inner connectedness, that inner knowingness at all times. Faith is that shred of memory that keeps you connected and guides your flight through the clouds of life.

I am your Angel of Faith fully present and active on Earth, available for all who will accept my assistance. Freely I offer my gifts of faith to be fully connected and know this single stranded connection is your guide line to God.

You come into Earth's density knowing forgetfulness will shroud your awareness quickly, and with this safety line of faith to see you through, to assist you until that time in development when the veils drop away and you know God as yourself again.

I am your Angel of Faith. Accept my assistance to realize your faith is there. Accept my hand to embrace your safety line as you move about life. Open your heart and mind enough to call on me. Have only enough faith to give me a try. In fullness of faith in you, I am at your service. I am Erehdenael. Give me a try! ✿

Erehdexael
Angel of Faith

Akenisael

Angel of Forgiveness

A s distasteful and unpleasant memories of long past occurrences resurface, call me, your Lady of Forgiveness, to assist in transmuting these energies to Love, to release the hold that these memories have on you. Many of you now will feel these memories calling and pushing you to complete this process, so you can move on to your present activities in the Light.

As these memories clamor for your attention, as if refusing to remain buried deep within, *you choose* what you do about them. You may continue to try to bury them, delaying change, and refusing to accept responsibility for your reality. Or you may begin your personal house cleaning of these old emotional scars and memories, knowing that forgiveness is the first step in healing yourself and your reality.

I am Akenisael (*a ken nee' siy el'*), your Angel of Forgiveness, and I can help you let go and heal your scars, understand and even accept the past as OK, and forgive yourself and all others for your (and their) roles in these dramas. I can help you know that you lived through all events of your past by your choice and your own design, to learn the needed lessons and gather the emotional harvest that you desire for this life on Earth.

Feel the truth of this, even as you feel the pain and sorrow inside of yourself. Breathe through the sadness and guilt and all the other gripping emotions stored deep inside, opening to the possibility of releasing the hold that these emotions have held

akenisael
Angel of Forgiveness

over you. These old scars, old emotional programs are still running your life, directing and choosing for you, as if you are still the child who incurred these hurts. This continues even if you are not conscious of it, until these wounds are healed.

Forgiveness is letting go of the past and being fully present, knowing that you (and everyone else) did the best you could at the time. Your intentions were the best that you could have had at the time, completely right for the lesson that you had decided to work on and possibly complete.

You literally magnetized the events and situations into your life that were needed to understand, learn and grow physically, emotionally, mentally, and spiritually. Time now is accelerating, even as the frequencies are accelerating on Earth. You are in the time of transition, and the law of grace now in effect for humanity will assist in transmuting your past far more quickly, *if* you choose to forgive and let go of the past.

If you *choose* forgiveness for yourself and all others, you can be in peace now, radiating peace fully and gloriously. Forgiveness is letting go of the past and being fully present, regardless of the past or possible future. I, Your Angel of Forgiveness, can help you with this, if you but ask.

If you ask for this assistance and allow my help, I can facilitate your letting go of all of the emotions that are not love, and assist you in choosing love, appreciation, acceptance, and allowance. I can assist in the release of all of the hurts and pain of stuffed and frozen emotions. Allow my assistance and I will be your steadfast friend through the thick and thin of your changes, as you emerge into the loving embrace of God. Of course, you are already in the loving embrace of God, but you will know it and feel it after forgiving yourself and all others.

Allow yourself to be with the old feelings that come up, and call on my help to release all emotional ties to them. Breathe deeply and feel them as you allow my assistance in forgiving yourself and all others for all energy exchanges of the past. Forgiveness brings a freeing release to be totally present, and feel great about yourself, the past and future, and all that is happening now.

I come to you with compassion and loving forgiveness. I am your Lady of Forgiveness, available for your request. I am Akenisael. ✿

Omlipon

Angel of Desire

D esire is God's tool, His voice to shift you, creating and moving, through life. The push of desire urges you onward, to choose and act, to manifest and create, and then choose again. Desire is the rubberband of school house Earth, pulling you onward, motivating and propelling you through life, helping you maintain movement.

I am Omlipon, (*om' li pon'*) your Angel of Desire, offering my assistance in recognizing and acknowledging desires, and moving with them in a constructive, beneficial manner.

As an early and essential step in the creation process, accurately focused and aligned desire, fervently embraced and coupled with appropriate action yields satisfying results. Desire has gotten 'bad press' over the years, and yet this is an essential aspect of life on Earth: free will and freedom of choice. It is the motor in the engine of life, the driving force for change. It is the energy that inflates and supports choice.

Everyone has desires, and more clearly when open and connected to God within you, when living Truth, being real. Often the children of God are taught to deny their truth, to deny the driving force within them, without any constructive outlet to fulfill these suppressed desires.   Parents suppress desires within themselves, and their children act them out. As parents and teachers, you pass on your legacy of unfulfilled desires when you sit in denial of this driving force of creation without resolution at the time of the desire.

Using the first or at least an early window of opportunity to fulfill your desires, creates in the moment. Trying to fulfill your latent wishes later in life through your children is to make choices for them, creating further dramas to unravel in life, and further need for resolution.

As children of parents with suppressed desires, you have conflicted desires as you proceed through life carrying this legacy of your predecessors. Allow my assistance to come in touch with your own desires and find beneficial ways of fulfilling these.

Desire is a precious gift of God! Accept this direct line of communication from God and begin to move and breathe, to feel your own desires. I offer my assistance to feel and know them, then move with these inner desires in fulfilling scenarios of relief and joy. Open your heart and mind to trust your desires and God, then move in the creational dance of life.

I am Omlipon, your Angel of Desire, available to assist all who ask in knowing what you want, and honoring your desires in beneficial ways that support and fulfill you while considering the whole. ✿

Omlipon
Angel of
Desire

Jehmorael

Angel of Thinking

As you think, you create. Conscious thought, with fervently held, clear intent, creates desired results. Thinking is synonymous with creating at more subtle levels. Whether you, as the thinker and creator, are thinking while subtle or not, your thoughts are definitely creating. Know that every thought is created in form somewhere.

Every thought creates a reality, whether within you or someone else or elsewhere. A thought by anyone within a relationship will resound and rebound within that relationship, creating as it moves. It will be felt and will manifest in some form.

With this knowledge comes responsibility to acknowledge your thoughts, to know that you create every moment of your existence, to process your desires, and be intentional with your thinking.   You as humans have not been taught how to think. You entertain many random thoughts constantly without regard for their effect in creation.

Thoughts *are* heard by creation, and are acted upon. Make no mistake. As a human you may be deaf to others' thoughts, but all of Earth and creation hear and react to thoughts. As your Angel of Thinking, I, Jehmorael (*jah mo' riy el'*), offer my assistance to help you manage your thoughts, to bring awareness to the process.

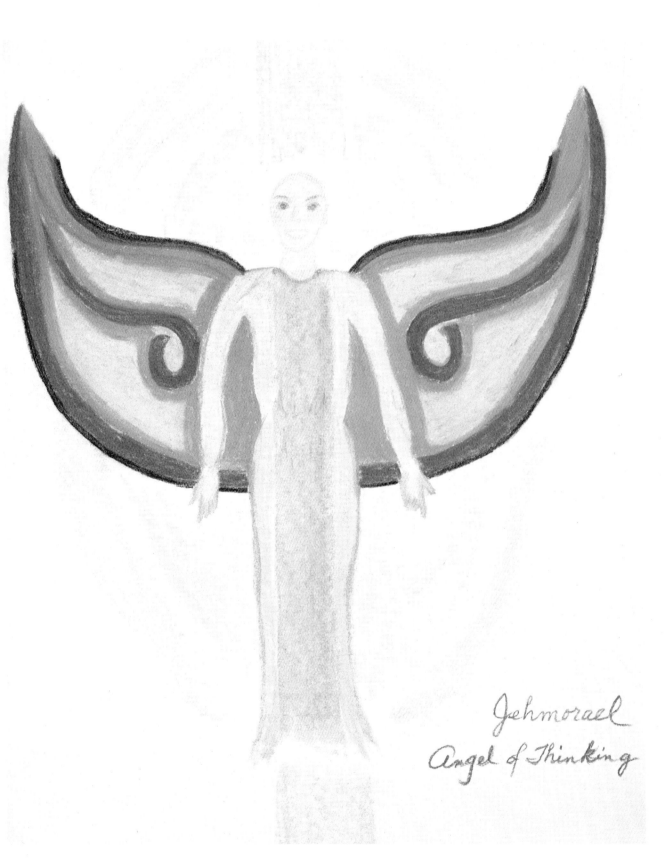

Jehmorael
Angel of Thinking

Deliberate thinking with clear intent, nurtured with fervent desire, creates desired results. This you are capable of now and are doing, with varied results, due to the lack of conscious thought.

Another capacity humans have and are largely unaware of is that of knowingness. You are all 'wired' for it, but few of you are consciously accessing the ability. Ask and I will assist you in unfolding and using this ability of knowingness.

Humanity is essentially a telepathic race, still sending out thoughts without consciously receiving them. The volume is wide open without regard for the listeners' 'ears.' Now with these higher frequency energies bathing the Earth and humanity, as a race you are moving back to being consciously telepathic with clear reception including all five senses plus emotions.

You are already sending thoughts and feelings, so now you will be able to do this consciously with clear intent, focus and purpose, with the exchange that will complete the cycle.

In a telepathic interaction with clear exchange, you will come to know the *faux pas* you have created with the rest of creation. Yet this has been understood and accepted to now, as a parent accepts a child's tottering steps as the earnest efforts of learning. As the child grows and matures, he is expected to stand on his own. So, too, are you expected to learn and accept responsibility of communicating with your full abilities and sensitivity.

Accept the responsibility of this ability and understand that portions of it are active now. I, Jehmorael, offer my assistance in understanding this and getting a handle on what to do with it. Give me a call. I come with a thought. ✿

Sekoisie

Angel of Divine Will

Divine Will is God guiding. As your Angel of Divine Will, I, Sekoisie (*seh koy' see'*), am available to assist you in realigning with God's Will and your own Divine plan for life.

Have you reached a block or barrier in life that would not budge regardless of what pressures you applied, only to relax and have it all work out splendidly? This is Divine Will at play as you step out of your controlling role. Divine intervention and assistance can be your everyday experience if you only invite this into your life. A lack of harmony indicates a need for change. A lack of flow and ease is created by your resistance to Divine input in your life. Invite the serenity to receive, hear and move with Divine Will.

As humans, you may have noticed your restricted field of vision, your lack of awareness of the options available or the situations being orchestrated in your life. You are not alone in this life, but are part of a team. You in your body, your ego sense of who you are, may see only what is obvious in front of you, but you are indeed a part of a larger team, including your Higher Self, your personal connection to God. Allow this team work and God to play a part in your life.

Open to Divine guidance and allow Divine Will to assist you in movement, growth, and change. Allow, accept, and appreciate this gift of God's touch in your life. Allow for the possibility and probability that He knows more of the options open to you than you do. Accept that He is always available and providing Divine Will to guide your choices and decisions. Open your heart to appreciate His Love of all that you are, of every step you take, and of all the outcomes you achieved, each valuable and precious to Him. Divine Will is available to all of humanity as you allow, accept, and appreciate this gift of God, the secret ingredient of all achievements in life.

I am Sekoisie, your Angel of Divine Will, ready and willing to assist you in inviting Divine Will into your life. I can assist you in allowing Divine Will to play a role in guiding your creations of reality in ease and grace. I am God's agent to assist in Divine Will. I invite your call. ✿

SeKoisie
Angel of Divine Will

Astonae

Angel of Ascension

Celestial energies are pouring into the Earth's atmosphere now, bathing all of humanity with the needed energies for growth and ascension. These energies, gifts of God's Love, are vibrant in frequencies of change, truth, new patterns of behavior, new concepts and principles. Change is being accelerated at ever increasing rates for all on Earth.

Many relationships and situations will move into change now. All are being given these gifts of acceleration, and many of you are *accepting and applying* these transformative energies to effect change and complete lessons of life. Success will become the norm in your life, as you will feel more energized and incredibly more effective in your endeavors.

Individuals grow and learn through a myriad of different lessons. Most will change at different rates and many will grow in different directions. Relationships will necessarily change and evolve with growing appreciation of the diversity and change in others. Some will take more time to acknowledge the need for change and access the gift of transformative energies.

Compassionate and understanding team members will assist in these decisions when asked and allowed. All are allowed free will to change and grow at their chosen

Astonae,
Angel of
Ascension

rate. At this time all on Earth have free will and *are choosing*, whether consciously, by default, or unconsciously. No decision *is in itself* a decision.

These gifts of transformative energies are welcome and comforting, as well as invigorating for those who decide to learn and grow, move and change. These energies will be mightily uncomfortable for those who stringently hang on to the past and refuse change in this time. There is no safety in stagnation now. At the time of birth of an infant, non-movement would be fatal. So also is this your time of birth. So grow and move, change and go with the push of birth into Ascension.

I am Astonae (*as' toe nay'*), your Angel of Ascension, your messenger of God's gifts of change, here to assist in all matters of ascension. At your request, I am with you, assisting in knowing, growing, breathing, changing - all steps of birth into higher frequency dimensions.

Ascension is happening every day now, step by step. Even the Earth is in her ascension. Her frequencies are increasing with every day. Changes abound and will continue with greater frequency as the Earth completes her birth process into higher dimensions. Her hope is that humanity can ascend with her.

Ascension is the goal of the growth process on Earth. As you grow in understanding and benevolence, in compassion and connectedness, your awareness opens to know your link to all of creation. This doorway of awareness opens your heart, mind, and soul to communion with your brothers and sisters on all levels. Your priorities begin to shift, and you choose gradually to step into another reality of existence. You become aware of and open to the rest of your team, those Ascended Ones who cluster around you, eager to assist you in growth and comfort you on your path.

These are experiences of ascension, that are reflective of your concurrent physical transition. Your physical body also is growing in Light as you shed your layers of armor and speak your truth, as you let more Light flood your body and radiate from your Being.

Many of you installed layer upon layer of protective shielding as you went through your lives. This allowed you to address life on its terms - that of lower, more dense frequencies - resulting in forgetfulness of how to reconnect and operate on the finer, higher frequencies of Light. As your Light builds in strength and brightness, as the Love of God radiates through and from your heart, the layers of armor will drop away, no longer needed or wanted, as you flow in the joy and freedom of your Light Body.

Maintaining your connection to the Light and Love of God without your armor in trying situations is the new pattern of life as the body transforms more and more into the Light Body. Your body, mind, and heart may feel tender as you drop your armor, vulnerable and naked, as you step into your truth and allow others their choices and truths. Your radiant Light Body will grow in strength and brilliance as you trust and allow, remaining connected to God. Gradually let go of your control mechanisms, your continuous adjustments of your environment and situation, and trust, breathing in the Light and Love of God.

Thus you ascend, step by step, level by level, radiating the Love, Light, and Wisdom of God. It's part of God's plan that all three-dimensional races ascend. The human races of Earth are in transition, approaching your time of completion. I offer my assistance in your acknowledgment of this truth now. I offer my help in every step along the way, for strength, understanding, gentleness, comfort, and joy in change. Open to me and ask. I will attend immediately in joyful haste. I am Astonae, your Angel of Ascension, at your service. ✿

Lehjolei

Angel of Comfort

omfort for the soul, heart, mind and physical body is brought forth on healing wings of love by the Angel of Comfort. I am Lehjolei (*lej' sho la'*), sent by God to comfort you. Many of you feel the pain of separation in spirit as well as heart, feel abandoned and forgotten, suffer the heartache and anguish of soul break. Many of you have lost your way and have no comfort to console you. So many of you grind your teeth in sorrow and loneliness with no one to comfort you. All of you who suffer these and the physical torment of illness, allow my ministrations, to soften your trials.

I come with the grace and blessings of God's comfort. Ask and I will assist all you who suffer the inner anguish and pain of the downward spiral, out of control. Let me caress your heart, soften your path, gentle your soul with my loving ministrations. I come to you with open arms, with wings to enfold and uplift you to the pure comfort of a mother's arms and father's hugs.

Open your heart to allow me to comfort you in your agony of despair. I know your pain and walk with you as you stumble. I can lift you as you fall. Open your mind to my offer to soften the pressures of your unwieldy load. I come to you in love and joy. Let me help you see again past the twisting pain of anguish. I can soften the

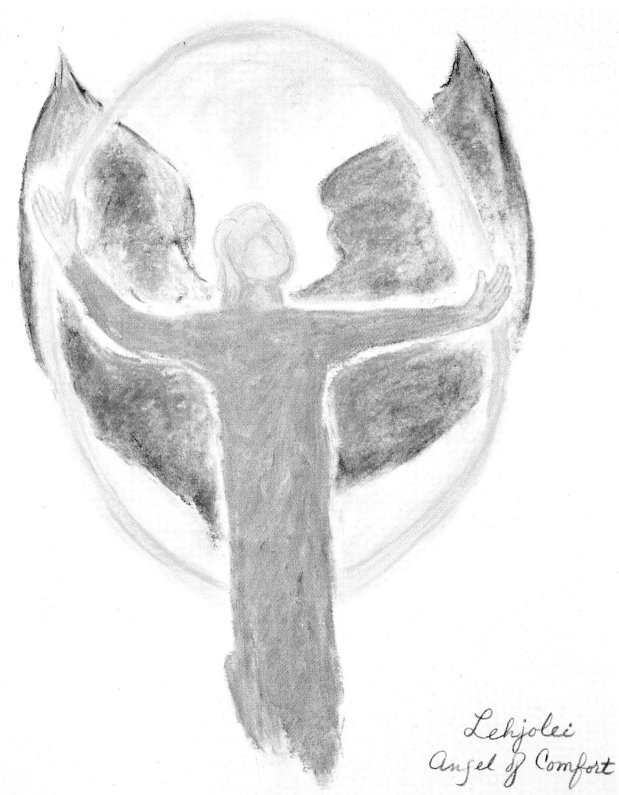

Lehjolei
Angel of Comfort

grip of these and other emotions, physical ailments, and spiritual sorrows, if you but ask for and allow my help.

Open your heart and mind to my offer to help you. Call me any time to soften your load and bring you comfort. The gentle relief of my comfort helps you breathe again, smile again, embrace life again. Call me to assist with discomfort of any kind. I gladly offer my comfort to all who ask. Your comfort is my greatest joy. ✿

. . . breathe, smile, embrace life again . . . in the grace and blessings of God's comfort.

~Angel Lehjolei.

Holmisei

Angel of Life

I am Holmisei (*hol ma say*), your Angel of Life, of giving and receiving, of sharing and flowing with all of creation, of being part of this grand life experience.

Life on Earth can be a challenge to say the least. You arrived here and immediately forgot, descending into the density of polarities and duality. You lost awareness of your Divine connection, and felt abandoned and forgotten. Fear welled up inside of you, boosted by many around you, struggling with the game of life on Earth.

Yet the only way through this game is *to play the game,* participate in it fully, winning through the muck and emotionality of life here through experience. I, the Angel of Life, Holmisei, offer you assistance in being in life, fully and joyfully, with understanding and acceptance.

Many on Earth until now have chosen to be the observer, waiting for a perfect time to enter the game of life, waiting to be better prepared, looking for a better situation, unhappy with life in general. Abstaining from life does not gain experience for you or contribute to the whole. Many opportunities are presented to take part in life, yet these often go unnoticed, as you sit on the sideline of life, wondering, unaware, or really searching for the activity that resonates with you.

Holmisei
Angel of Life

I, Holmisei, am here to facilitate you getting into the game of life again. You may have lost your desire to participate. I can boost your desire to play in life with gusto! Open to my energetic assistance to join this dance of life again, to be in life here and now. Allow my assistance to choose your part, see and feel your opening to dive in, and play it fully. Call on my energies to help open many doors of opportunity to participate.

My energies include sharing and are much more even than this, for to share there must be a giver and a receiver, and in truth, both are each. In giving much is received. In accepting the role of receiver, much is given. A recipient is given to the giver, someone to receive his gift, as a gift to the giver. The interaction between both is essential to create the cycling of sharing.

As you interact, playing and dancing with others, many truths of self unfold within, which would otherwise remain dormant. If you are bored or feeling unhappy, in a damaging situation, and in need of change, look for the doorways of opportunity to participate in life in different ways.

Call me, your Angel of Life, to assist in creating these doorways of opportunity, recognizing them as they appear, then choosing and accessing each chosen door fully. Your call is my command even as I am your opportunity. ✿

Peikule

Angel of Brotherhood

Many of you are now longing for your families, feeling empty because you have no close friends, and feeling distanced and out of *sync* with your families of birth. This desire for family is the pull to be with your family of like frequency, your family of like resonance. You feel the tug, the urgency to find these brothers and sisters, begin living and working together, each caring, and supporting, and loving the other.

Many of you have old emotional programs that keep you aloof, separate from others, unable to enjoy the loving togetherness of friends and family. Those of you with this old programming, locked in the anguish of separation, are mostly veiled from your separation within yourself. I, Peikule (*peh koo lay*), your Angel of Brotherhood, can assist you in opening to and appreciating yourself and then another.

Call for my assistance to help release this old programming. Open to my assistance as you come to love and appreciate yourself, opening to your self worth and value, as you come to know you have much to offer others in friendship. Send my loving ministrations to those other souls that cry in the anguish of aloneness. I bring energies that unite, that help one help another, appreciate a brother, grow into units, groups of people who are families of enormous size, growing, teaching, sharing, loving, all flowing back to Oneness.

I am your Angel of Brotherhood. Allow me to help heal the scars and pains of separation and abandonment. Let me help you reach out to another with hope and love in your heart. I can soften the emotions that bind and restrict your gentleness, your desire to love. Invite my energetic help to soften a rift, cement relationships, boost camaraderie, and generate the glow of love in your life.

Let me help you appreciate the unity already present in your life and spur these relationships on to greater perfection. Let me open your eyes and heart to the perfection in another. I am the Angel of family living, of sisterhood, of groups of friends, of neighborly energies, of groups united in common purpose for the growth and evolution of humanity.

I come with the openness and joy of hugs and caresses, dancing and flowing, connecting and supporting. This support is not usually 'doing it for you' type assistance. The togetherness of your real family will be a healthy relationship in which members joyfully work together, each doing his or her part.

I bring the energies of coming together. Let me assist your group, whether couple, family, friends, workers in a company, a nation. My magic helps people love themselves and one another and appreciate the grand gifts of nature. Mother Earth is indeed a grand feminine energy and long has she needed humanity's appreciation and reciprocal caring.

All strive for growth and unfoldment and then realize the joy of helping others grow. These are all steps back to Oneness. I am your Angel of Brotherhood, here to assist all who desire brotherhood, oneness with your real family, unity in diversity on Earth. Call me for loving assistance and joyful help back to unity. ✿

Peikule
Angel of Brotherhood

Muriel

Angel of Simplicity

S|implicity is bare essence, the distillate of spirit. When in doubt, simplify. I, Muriel (*moo rey el*), am your Angel of Simplicity, here now to help you and all of humanity relax, breathe deeply and see this essence in everything, everyone, every moment. I can help you see the beauty, the art of simplicity. Simplicity in art maintains balance and alignment, and is little more than a symbol conveying the pure essence.

The simple approach can be and often is far more powerful and effective, almost miraculously so. Simplicity most directly connects to the Divine. 'Keep it simple' rarely fails to give superb results. Allow the intellect to rest, and spirit will direct you to 'simple.' This approach works as a road map through life, if you allow it.

Call me, Muriel, your Angel of Simplicity, available to help you with simple powerful answers. With your permission I can assist you in far reaching changes as you just simplify. You often think life is hard, expect complicated steps to solutions, and with these thoughts, you create it. Try thinking simple, looking for the simplest possible answer and expect to find it. With your permission, I'll gladly assist you in creating simplicity.

Open your mind to the simple way, and your heart will gladly follow. I am your Angel of Simplicity here to help you see the simple solution, to help you go the simplest route, to help you breathe easy and relax into simplicity.

My message is simple. I offer simplicity, pure and simple. When life feels too complicated, and your energy can't keep up with the pace, call me. When life overwhelms you, call on my energies for relief. I am Muriel. It's simple. ✿

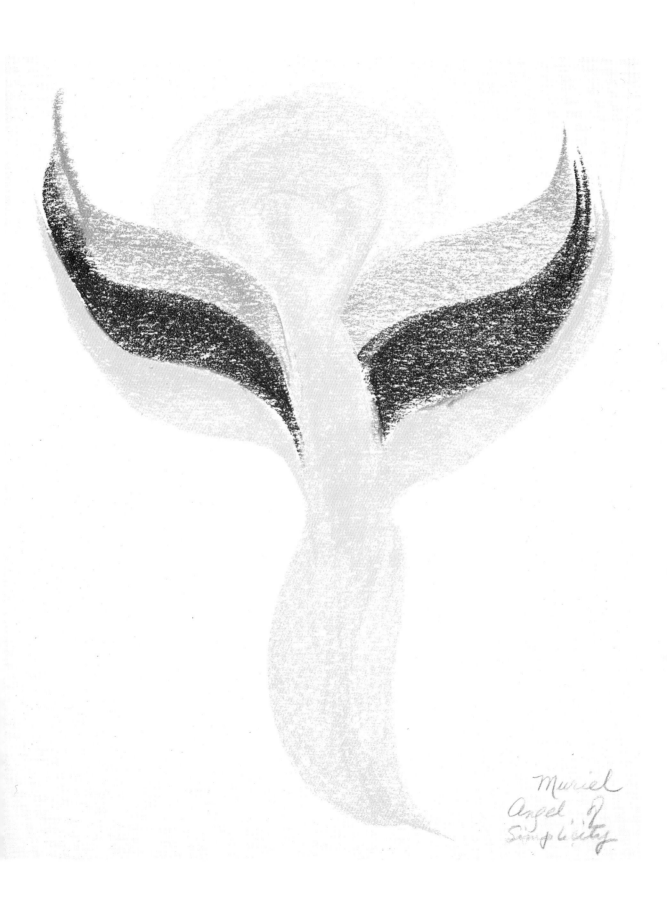

Muriel
Angel of
Simplicity

Hilojael

Angel of Cooperation

Y our world has been operating for generations with competition as a primary motivation. Now, with the higher frequences bathing the Earth and shifting your realities, *cooperation is beginning to replace competition* as a dominant operating procedure. It is mindful to note that many of *you* are now choosing to assist others, choosing life supporting activities that support the whole instead of considering the self only. This trend will continue to increase in strength and become the norm on Earth.

Cooperation will be seen in areas unheard of in the past. Previously diverse opponents are beginning to accept each other for who and what they are, and move into cooperative activities that benefit all and harm none.

Polarities are actually strengthening now, each side becoming stronger as repetitive and increasingly powerful energies bathe the Earth. Loving acceptance of yourself and another's strength of expression and other choices, without judgment or other base emotions, will provide the continued opportunities for constructive interactions. This openness and acceptance also supports the overall increase of frequencies for all involved. The resultant integration of the life supporting aspects of these new energies benefits everyone.

Hilojael
Angel of Cooperation

The challenge now is not *if* you will do good works, but *how* strong, assertive people can work together harmoniously, effectively and joyfully. Many final lessons will surface as you attempt to share your wisdom, create together, and be a family.

You will have lessons like how to consider others' contributions along with your own, and how to honor the purpose of the group above your own agendas. Sometimes, in your fervor to continue, you may forget to cooperate, so caught up are you in achieving your set goals. You may need to take responsibilities for your own personal growth needs, so you can be an effective member of the group.

Lessons of respect, allowing and acknowledging another, appreciating another, supporting another, and loving one another *and yourself* will be a part of cooperation. Living and working together cooperatively will yield an abundant harvest, if you will embrace the great opportunities cooperation affords you.

As you move into cooperative groups, to live and work and play, and issues arise inside (*and they will!*), feel these deeply buried and long forgotten emotions that rear their faces again. If you allow yourselves to feel these, wave upon wave, you *have begun* your cooperative, healing process inside. This is cooperation with and within yourself, responding to your need and desire to be effective in cooperative interactions.

If you have some questioning within yourself about how to cooperate and *if* you are cooperating effectively, then feel the rightness of the moment, feel for the joy within the creation. Are you open and flowing your energies within yourself? If your mind or heart or soul is pushing up some strong emotions of the past, use this moment for the opportunity to heal within. Breathe through any constrictions inside and feel the residual emotions, blessing and nurturing this part of yourself. Be with this process as long as it takes.

I, Hilojael (*hi low jiy el),* your Angel of Cooperation, will assist you with this process, with your permission. Allow the nurturing energies to irradiate and energize you, to flow into the areas where you stored these memories and emotions. Be gentle with this inner part of yourself that calls for healing now, that asks for a moment of cooperation within yourself.

As you feel these emotions, allow yourself to accept that you did the best you could at the time, and lovingly bless these situations of the past and the individuals who participated in these activities; bless and release them and yourself, grateful for the experience, happy for the opportunity to complete (hopefully) another lesson. Self acceptance and appreciation, established in your own sense of self worth and value, are necessary basics of your relationships, releasing you to appreciate the diversity and uniqueness of others.

As you complete and move on to *how* to work together for the common good, you will move from competition into cooperation in all aspects. The strong energies bombarding Earth now demand and support this change. What will be for the good of all individuals and the whole? The search for this answer will be a driving force now among all of Earth's peoples.

Cooperation, working together cooperatively, including and consulting with your team on how to best proceed for the desired results, is a choice. *Often the synergy of the entire team will create outcomes far in advance of what you can achieve alone.*

To work joyfully and successfully with your team, you may still need to let go of self-satisfying needs, your need to own your contributions, see an outcome as solely your gift. This letting go of a need to own an outcome, and then becoming a working part of the team with the benefit of the whole as top priority, is cooperation at the level required now.

As you let go of the need for self-satisfying results, you open to the need of the whole. Often what you thought of as menial before will be the job needing attention. 'Whatever it takes' becomes the directive. All energies woven into a project become part of the final fabric and, therefore, all contributions are equally important and equally appreciated.

Becoming part of a team means wholeness, like an organ is part of the body. The needs of the body must be considered before the desires of the organ. Cooperation is a balance of each team member considering the whole above self while supporting self and other team members in Being. The group becomes One.

Openness and honesty in interactions, accepting and allowing diversity, while addressing issues will assist in continuing the flow of cooperation. Many of these issues will bring up strong emotions, often unrelated to the issues at hand. An accepting, open minded and open hearted team will allow and support the truth being spoken. This may feel like disruption and delay; however, it will assist with the continuing flow of the team -- without this clearing, your team will surely stalemate and disband.

Frequently issues will take some time to resolve. Patience and understanding, allowing another's choices are imperative in cooperation. Continuing cooperation will require ongoing honest expression, allowing others' choices, appreciating diversity, and a desire to maintain the whole. Occasionally non-doing will be required as you gauge your contribution to a relationship or a project.

Cooperating with your Higher Self offers an effective training ground for cooperative living. Your Higher Self is your direct line to God, with the Angels just expressions of Him, even as you are an expression of Him. Turn to your Higher Self and invite this guidance into your life. Once this becomes an operating, cooperative relationship, your ability to participate cooperatively in all of life will vastly improve.

Cooperation is a grand challenge for humankind today. It provides continuous opportunity to take a stand and express your truth, assist others, support the greater good, and move toward accepting responsibility for your world as part of your reality.

Cooperation brings the joy of working in unison, provides the opportunity for the families of like resonance to come together in life supporting works and joys. A home going - coming!

As your Angel of Cooperation I gladly offer my assistance to help you come into acceptance within yourself, to know how to work and play cooperatively with others, including your teams on other realms. Invitingly, I await your call. I am Hilojael. ✿

Miru

Angel of Unity

I am Miru (*meh roo*), the Angel of Unity come forth to assist all on your way Home. Many of you feel the lack of completeness, a reflection of forgetting your Oneness. All desire completion; it is humanity's driving force, though few of you recognize the core issue of desires in life. Only Oneness with God brings complete joy and happiness, completion that is complete.

In living your lives on Earth, you have denied your body and Beingness much experience, even as the experience gathering continues. You denied yourself experiences in the hope of maintaining or reestablishing your connection to God. Whether these methods were effective or not, these old patterns of behavior are being replaced. The new methods coming into your reality to satisfy needs and desires are nestled in Oneness and what is good for the whole.

Now physical health, tone, and resiliency have become more important to maintaining clarity and flexibility of Being. The value of many activities is being re-evaluated, and the resultant choices are leaning toward activities that maintain or increase consciousness and bring more fulfillment to soul and the whole, these being One.

No force. Coercion is not used. Activities that did bring satisfaction, or at least relief, no longer do. So these are being examined and new steps are being taken, new choices considered, preferences examined as to outcomes. Old habits drop away. New behaviors emerge. New thinking and exchanges occur.

The lower self gradually becomes aware of and allows some input from the Higher Self, is gratified with the results, and thus continues and encourages this relationship. The lower self begins to trust, and to appreciate the assistance of the Higher Self. Gradually the lower self asks for and accepts, desires and gets constant Higher Self guidance, trusting God and the Oneness within.

This constant association grows in appreciation and becomes a loving exchange; in the Oneness, separation becomes a thing of the past. You live constantly connected, clear and open to feelings, thoughts, sensations, inspirations, and knowingness.

In this state, the love, wisdom, and power of the Higher Self are shared in totality with the lower self, as the lower self turns to the Higher Self for guidance in all aspects of life. The lower self recognizes itself as an aspect of the totality and completely surrenders to this union.

At this time of surrender and loving appreciation, the Higher and lower selves feel a oneness that may become, by choice of the lower self, a physical oneness. The Higher Self is located in physicality, though less dense, over the lower self which inhabits the physical human body.

At the request of the lower self, and as the appropriate events converge to bring all energies of each into readiness, the Higher Self actually lowers Itself over the physical body of the lower self and merges in totality, this One now being Christed.

This merging may occur time and time again until the physical body has become aligned and balanced to the higher frequencies now coursing through it. The merged presence of the Higher Self is maintained longer and longer as the physical body grows in clarity and radiance, the mental body accepts this unity, and the emotional body vibrates in loving appreciation of this Gift of God.

In this merged state of Oneness, the knowledge and joy of the Higher Self become that also of the (previous) lower self. The understanding and joy of Oneness with and of God is known. The radiance and resonance of this Christed One are now a joy to behold and experience.

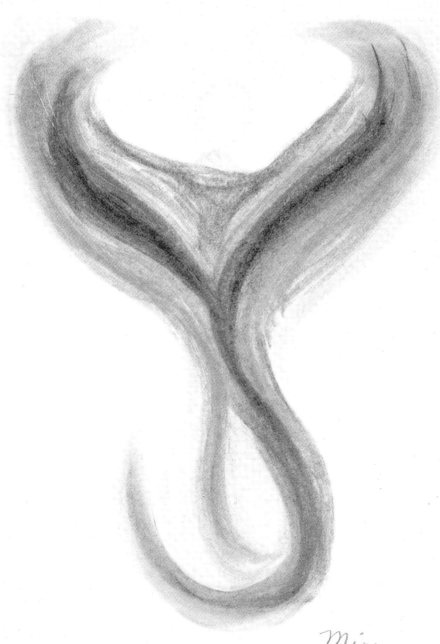

Miru
Angel of Unity

The very presence of a Christed Being on Earth thrills creation into joyful enthusiasm. Other individuals are a part of this thrilled creation, as the very resonance of a Christed Being brings waves of change to all around Him.

All of humanity have this choice of Oneness now. The higher frequencies bathing Earth now bring the energies for all to open and participate in this experience of Oneness again. You all have Higher Selves just waiting for recognition and reconnection. Your Higher Selves are your direct link to God, accepting the higher frequencies of Love and Light from God, and adjusting them to acceptable tones for you to receive and use.

I am your Angel of Unity here to help you realize that your Higher Self awaits your call, patiently and constantly. At your request I can assist you in knowing and living the joy of reunion with that Higher part of yourself. Erase the loneliness in your life by re-accepting the rest of Yourself.

Call to your Higher Self. Ask for only *your* Higher Self, of your consciousness, your body in this time and location. Be certain to get a 'yes' to these questions. Then ask for guidance and unity with God.

Ask. You must ask. Even your Higher Self has a 'hands off' policy toward you, unless you ask. Ask in reverence and expectancy, keeping your line open to hear the answers. Allow the quiet time regularly in you life to hear the answers. *Ask* and you shall receive.

Your Angel of Unity, I am again active on Earth to assist in your reunion with Your Self. I, Miru, offer to assist you in reconnecting back to God, remembering this connection, via your Higher Self, your direct connection to God. Welcome Home! ✿

Jarael

Angel of Diversity

T he grand plan for those of Earth is growth through a myriad of experiences, flowing back into Oneness at completion, and to whatever extent you are able during your lifetimes on Earth.

Your lives and roles on Earth are many and various. Diversity is maintained for an interesting variety of roles and for flow and movement. Should you be all alike, there would be few choices of roles, and thus boredom. Were you all alike, snug and content for life, you would have few shifts and little movement to maintain equilibrium, thus few opportunities for lessons.

The fact is diversity provides an incredible variety of choices and options, much to appreciate in the multitude of paths available to arrive at similar goals. Diversity in other people(s) reveals unsuspected ways of being and doing, of living and growing. Different races, with a myriad of looks and varying customs, embody a broad spectrum of strengths and qualities, all creating a beauty unique unto themselves. There is no right or wrong here, just different creations.

As you grow through your many lifetimes of challenges and opportunities, grow in knowing yourselves as the creators of your reality, your appreciation of diversity around you grows also. The tendency to wish every thing around be your own reflection decreases, as your appreciation of the differences grows. You begin to see the Master's touch of genius in the varieties of life's situations, interactions, and opportunities which are available as building blocks for your reality.

I am Jarael (*jah rae el)*, your Angel of Diversity, set in motion to assist you in understanding and valuing this diversity, then enjoying the playground of life, this astounding work of genius from God.

I offer you the choice of understanding and appreciating those different from you, those who choose other ways and customs, who perhaps choose opposing views of life. I offer you assistance in choosing to disagree and being disagreed with, to choose your own beliefs, and know and understand that these are uniquely yours. That others have the God given right to believe and be different, to live and feel differently, to create and evolve differently.

I offer you the joy of diversity and the splendor of uniqueness in your own right. You are different. No other person is exactly like you. Enjoy your own uniqueness, this gift of God's creational touch. You are unique and perfect right now. In the security of your own uniqueness, you can appreciate the diversity of others. In a moment you will be different, and yet still perfect.

Open your mind and heart to the joy of diversity within and without, in your life and all over the Earth. Open to the beauty of diversity. I offer my assistance now in accepting these truths and knowing this joy. I am Jarael, your Angel of Diversity. ✿

Jarael
Angel of Diversity

Kenije

Angel of Intuition

I am Kenije (*keh nee' jee'*), the Angel of Intuition, and I gift humanity with help in opening awareness, the ability to know an answer with just an introspective glance. Intuition is within the abilities of humanity, and yet has lain dormant in most until now.

Awaken now, dear friend, to your inner ability of knowing. Feel the gentle tickle of intuition as you question within. Open to the quiet whisper, the ever so gentle tug at the edge of your awareness. Many have active intuition and have just not known, not learned how to 'hear' it. For your intuition may speak to you in a number of ways.

Your surroundings will certainly speak to you, so that even with your outward stroke of attention, intuition catches your eye and awareness. With this flag, your attention opens within to the incoming information, gently allowing its unfoldment. At first, with your first times of working intentionally with intuition, the feel of the incoming information may be delicate. Just as you are ever so gentle with an unfolding flower, so touch on the unfolding information as it 'formulates' itself into recognizable form for your consciousness. Allow yourself to feel it, and you will know when to gently shift stronger attention to it. The information will become more focused, and you will feel the meaning, you will *know* it.

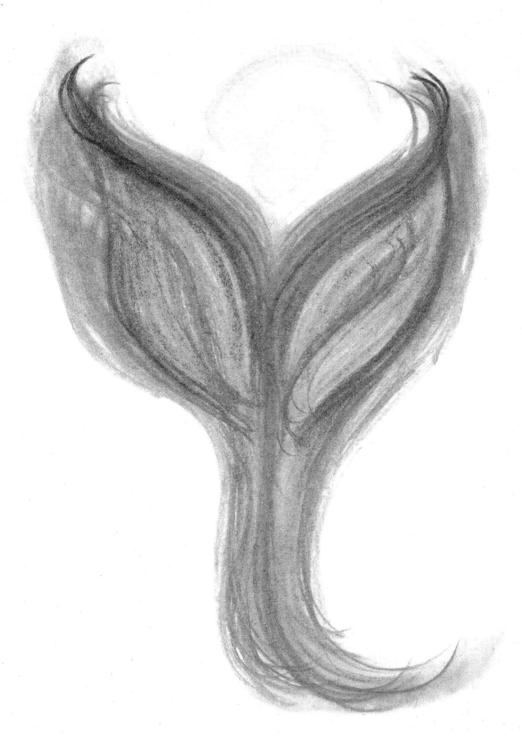

Kenija
Angel of Intuition

You may first feel it in your 'gut', as the solar plexus (the gut) *is* where you feel your knowingness. The 'hunch' is intuition tugging at your awareness. As ideas slip in and out of your mind, new ways to handle situations, this is active intuition assisting you on a daily basis.

As your Angel of Intuition, I am ready and available to assist you in your process of developing and learning to actively use this wonderful and blessed faculty. For indeed, it can be learned. All have this ability, and surely some individuals will always be more proficient than others. A little guidance and assistance can be very productive in boosting your abilities and heightening your perceptions.

I urge you to allow my assistance and encouragement of this unfolding talent. Also ask for answers to come to you. Ask, question within, and then release it. This release provides the gap of silence for the incoming answer. Ask, then be quiet to hear. A regular, quiet, introspective time is helpful in developing this intuitive connection.

I offer my help in opening your centers of intuition, for the higher aspect of yourself demands it. You are not this self same body alone, but are connected to a Higher Self that governs and guides this lower self. Allow me, dear friend, to help awaken your inner knowingness, that you may again be all that you were meant to be. Life becomes far easier with this intuitive connection reestablished and active. I offer this now to humanity to hasten your growth and lighten your load. Open to my gift and I will gladly assist you. I am your Angel of Intuition. ✿

Mohee

Angel of Emergence

T he challenge now is to live with the new energies and insights in balance, responding consciously rather than reacting on automatic to the shifts of energies within and without. With the shifting energies and growing awareness, you may feel as babes learning to walk and talk again, when you interact with others. For indeed interact with others you will!

Any changes in an equilibrium will require subsequent shifts to keep the balance. As you grow in strength and wisdom and love, so are many others also shifting and changing. Your temporary imbalances will bring up interesting opportunities as you come into awareness of how to move, think, and feel, and the effects these have on yourself and your environment.

What do you want? Think and feel your preference. Make clear choices. Choose your course consciously, opening to new outcomes and possibilities, rather than allowing old scenarios of reaction in lower energies to continually replay.

If your outcome does *not* appear the way you envisioned it, check for areas that need clarification. Speak your desires with care to others, knowing that they too are juggling new energies with great enthusiasm for their choices. *Share with care.* Be gentle, but firm; clear without sharpness in your choices and course corrections. Energize directions you choose and walk away from those you do not choose.

Allow. *Allow* others their choices and *make your own*. Strong energies will attract strong energies, so clear definitive choices will be imperative to continued movement with ease, comfort, and desired results.

As your powers increase so will your abilities of discernment. Use discernment and apply the insights given. Frequently you will need to turn on a dime, change directions abruptly, with your increasing insights and knowledge.

The energies of all of Earth, humanity included, are 'revving up.' You are being given the knowledge to move with great flexibility and speed, to become and direct these energies. You are being called upon to perform and complete great tasks on Earth now.

The choice is yours. Move with the new energies or try to hold your *status quo*. The latter will be difficult, for you have moved into a new age, resplendent with higher frequencies. Necessarily your inner self must shift to accommodate the dimensional shift of your world.

Move and play in these new energies and abilities. Become them. Feel the quickening energies of emergence and rejoice in them. Accept that a great change, a glorious and wondrous change is underway. Support and flow with this transition. Accept your legacy now.

Move into your Light Body. It is time to move and play in your Light Body, to rejoin the family of Light Beings that you are. Wake up time! Open your eyes, your awareness and come out of your dream. Emerge from your illusion of separateness and linear time and density.

Great masses of humanity are nearing this point of emergence now. Angelic assistance is but a call away. I, Mohee (*moe hee*), your Angel of Emergence, hover over and with you as you near this transition point to guard and protect you in this time of rapid change and increasing fluidity.

Changing your mind and heart decisions has become the prerogative of *all* of humanity now. It is your right and, indeed, your responsibility now to clearly monitor your preferences and move to create these. Your choices now will lean toward supporting and being part of the greater whole, rather than serving the self.

Long have I awaited this moment of emergence of humanity. Long have I tended your changes, protected your choices, and guarded your free will. I am your Angel of Emergence, available to assist as you emerge from your dreams in Earth's densities.

Mohee
Angel of Emergence

You are as a fledgling bird emerging from the cracked shell, or a newborn fresh from the womb, as you emerge into your new realities of higher dimensions with your new found abilities. I offer my assistance to ease your shift and strengthen your awareness of this process and these conscious choices.

I am your Angel of Emergence, assisting in changes occurring when your choices have become more clear and fewer, and you are aiming at and coming into enlightenment. My gifts are yours upon request, and joyfully are they given.
I am Mohee. ✿

Wake up time! Open your eyes, your awareness, and come out of your dream. Emerge from your illusion of separateness and linear time and density . . .

~Angel Mohee.

Segment Three

13 Angels

Angel of Honor, Voleczek
Angel of Fraternal Love, Tascabra
Angel of Ease, Janielle
Angel of Self Love, Kari
Angel of Innovation, Miklenael
Angel of Patience, Placidias
Angel of Protection, Unuliel
Angel of Peace, Escielle
Angel of Serenity, Mericu
Angel of Grace, Jemlien
Angel of Resonance, Derilicium
Angel of Benevolence, Haboine
Angel of Courage, Gilandriel

Voleczek

Angel of Honor

A s human beings continue to awaken, becoming increasingly aware of their Beingness with their multi-faceted abilities and faculties, many will desire to share these wonderful discoveries and the joy that they themselves feel. This desire to share is admirable and understandable.

"Does anyone else have this experience?" you may think. This is completely new to you, so surely others will want to hear about and experience this also. As your awareness unfolds, many other consciousnesses are also opening simultaneously. Others are having parallel experiences, though their specific experiences are as various as the individuals themselves.

Allow. Give others their space to unfold, and share on request. Honor their process and respect their experiences also, for theirs may well be as wonderful as your own. I am Voleczek (*voh' lehk zehk'*), your Angel of Honor, here to assist you in honoring others' choices and their free will to experience life as they choose.

Often in your zeal to share, you override another's choice, another's experience, even belittling it. Your intentions are well meant, though your results can be devastating. Open your awareness to another's process, beingness, and choices. Allow them to choose how they live and move and grow. Often you will discover in another fascinating aspects and wondrous creations, fully different from your own and fully valid and beautiful in their diversity.

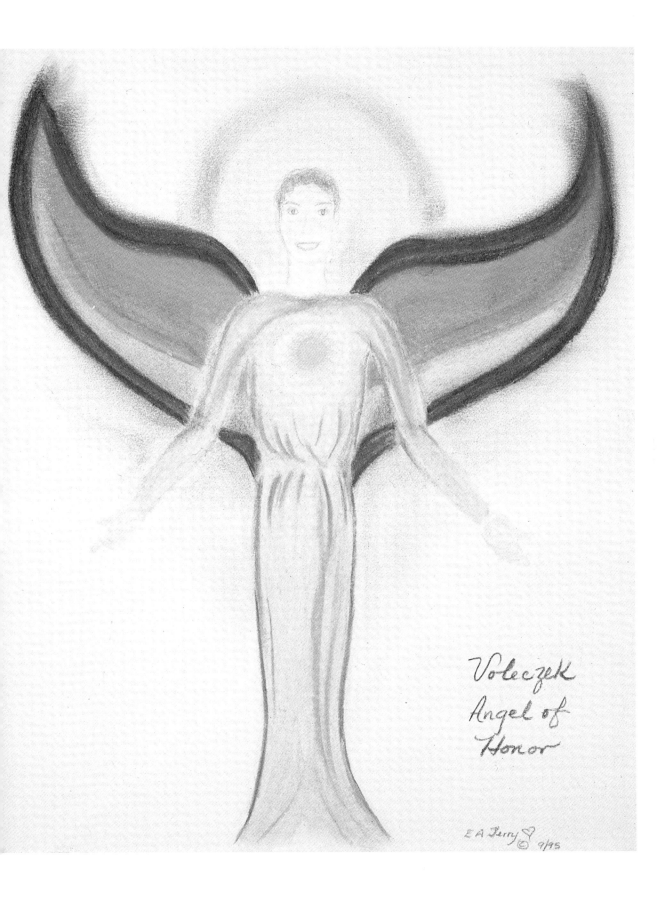

Voleczek
Angel of
Honor

E.A. Jerry♡
© 9/95

I am your Angel of Honor here to honor your process and assist you *when* called upon, for neither would I dishonor you and your choices. Always will I maintain a 'hands off' policy, except when you invite my assistance. I am available for pause, for a gentle realignment of your energies that you might appreciate another's initiative and creativity, another's will to create with their energies alone, or exclusive or inclusive of yours. Whatever their choices, certainly these choices will be their path and satisfy their need, a chosen lesson.

By honoring, you share an appreciation for another's initiative, another's choices, another's completions and striving. Often you may 'see' a better way, an easier way, and generously try to share this. To your surprise, the assistance may be rejected. Know that the intended receiver needed the lesson of doing, living life, of making his own choices. These activities are his education, and are necessary for his personal growth, evolution, and future activities.

At certain evolutionary levels sharing is needed and appreciated, even as we Angels are offering to cocreate you. Our team can be an intimate unit, depending on one another and appreciating each others' efforts. This team work happens often in life. You may not be a part of an individual's chosen team, or an individual may be soloing for a time.

Sharing and gifting are wonderful aspects of life everywhere. Allow another's choice to participate or abstain. This choice of another's is just that - his choice, which you may choose to honor. My gift is assistance in this area of discerning and honoring by allowing and appreciating.

My gift of honor is freely offered. You honor me by inviting my energies to be part of your team. I am Voleczek, at your service, your Angel of Honor. ✿

Tascabra

Angel of Fraternal Love

T he gift of becoming human is a divine gift with many beings vying for the opportunity and few receiving this honored role. To also be privileged to parent or teach a child on Earth is indeed a precious gift, one reflected deeply in the cherishing love of the parent and teacher. Deep within your being you know the specialness of this event and your great responsibility to nurture and love this child as you would yourself hope to have been loved.

All who are chosen and choose to be a child's nurturing guardian and guide feel the bond of love grow as the child innocently and exuberantly lavishes the parent/teacher/guide with his unconditional love. The joy of assisting another soul on his journey on Earth folds into the bliss of loving and guiding, as you blend wisdom with love and light, and gradually share this gift with the child for use and application on his journey.

Fraternal love ignites softly at the prospect of this nurturing role, unearthing many a buried issue to unravel and heal, as flashes of your own childhood experiences rise for resolution within your daily activities of the opposite role as adult guide to another soul. The fraternal love grows and softens your reactions, gradually opening your heart and mind to the gifts of the diverse experiences of life and the joys of loving.

As your perspective expands, your understanding and tolerance of others grow, opening you to allow your child, with your gentle guidance, to choose and apply his free will to his life. The child chooses and feels the results, chooses and feels the reaction. You gently guide, allowing the child his results.

I am Tascabra (*tahs cah' brah'*), your Angel of Fraternal Love, sent to Earth to help you as parents, teachers, guides and friends to understand, accept, appreciate, and perform your roles of guiding other souls here on Earth.

Fraternal love is a mature love with many levels of allowing and accepting, appreciating and caring, often with deep abiding love and wonder. It moves with a life of its own as the relationship of child and guide, child and teacher grows and expands.

You can surely see the obvious needs of the early nurturing of and caring for the infant. The soul embodying this infant is quite helpless at motor control and verbal expression of its needs. This part is simple and understandable, yet often fraught with unknowables.

Allow my assistance when you are at your wits end and need help. Ask my assistance for the complete knowledge of caring for this soul in joy, ease, and comfort. Open to my nurturing energies and ask that I foster your caring and understanding, your openness to the needs and desires of this child of God.

As the child grows and individuates, he will begin to realize his separateness from you. Open to the fostering of this aspect of individuality, nurturing his ability to choose and move, to create and express, to love and relate to others, to appreciate and nurture.

I offer my assistance with fraternal love, as the child in your care grows and differentiates, moving through the different stages of childhood. Each child is always unique, with each aspect of life lived differently. Allow my assistance to appreciate and validate the experiences of the child as an individual with his own creative ways of living.

Parenting and teaching can be a challenge since it is a 'learn on the job' situation. No one is fully prepared, or will know how to fulfill all needs, or even what the problem is sometimes as the relationships and choices evolve. Openly ask for my assistance and feel the insights dawn, the sureness return, the soothing energies of caring ease the situation at hand.

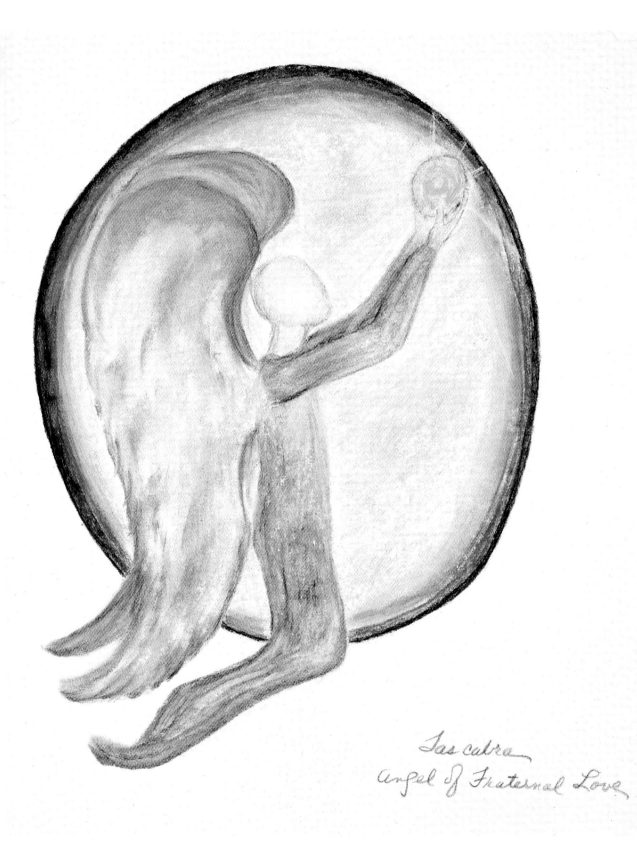

Iascabra
Angel Of Fraternal Love

I also offer my assistance in times of pain and sorrow, in joy and levity, in sickness and in health. I understand your concern and fears, your anguish and depression, your sadness and anger. Allow my assistance to soften and transmute these energies, to guide your hand and heart as you change and grow with your child. Open to God's caring concern and nurturing intentions. Allow the gentle energies of my angelic gifts to assist you in your caring and nurturing of another.

Open to the joy and wonder of life in fraternal love. Allow my assistance to continually grow and play, for you all grow together. Remember to play! I am Tascabra, eager to assist you in all matter of fraternal love. I await your request. ✿

Janielle

Angel of Ease

The Angel of Ease has joined you now to offer assistance. Humans, locked in the densities of Earth, make life hard. Old patterns, old programming tell humans how hard they must work to succeed, to accomplish their goals. So my first wave of energies as your Angel of Ease is to soften rigid belief systems that hold you prisoner to the past, that lock out the guidance of your Higher Self and your guides. Sluggish educational systems reinforce and build complicated structures to justify these partial truths, for indeed truth changes in each moment, as a reflection of an individual's growth of awareness.

New vistas open as you move with ease, and breathe deeply of the myriad possibilities offered in the bubbling seas of your awareness, gentle easy movements, flowing through life, your body's energy centers, or chakras, blossoming to energetically connect you to all of creation, to God, to God within you. Ease, the gift of God, dissolves illusions of time, of struggle, of hard work. Ease brings lightness, soft open hearts, gentle loving touches, and grand dances of creation, one with another and with all the kingdoms in creation.

I am Janielle (*jah' nee el'*), your Angel of Ease, here to soften the pressure of life. Long have you struggled in vain to achieve your goals, only to create more goals heaped upon those. Allow me to gentle your soul's struggle, to ease your heart's twisting pain, to soften your ideas of life's needs as you breath deeply and open your eyes and hearts to simpler ways.

Simplicity. Long complicated answers to life's demands can be distilled down to the simplest common answer with ease. Add my energies to your life. Call me as you awaken and as you lie down to rest, and I will gentle the currents and eddies of your surging soul. Open to my ministering gifts of ease, to the awareness that life can be easy, gentle, satisfying.

Many of you feel stifled by life's demands, unable to get ahead, questing for ways to 'succeed' and looking forward to a time of peace and tranquillity, of fulfillment. Call me now! Let me help you now, in this moment, to see life with ease, to live life simply and with joy. I am the great distiller of truth. I wipe away the illusions of struggle and pain.

All who are ready to exit the arena of struggle, choose my assistance now. Call on me, your Angel of Ease, and even now as you read these words, I will soften your inner knowingness to accept ease in life. You, dear soul, can continue to live in pain and struggle *or* create ease now. Call me. I will help now to ease your body, to bring ease of movement, ease of old emotional scars, ease of the pain in your soul. Ask and I answer.

It's easy! Just call. I am Janielle, your Angel of Ease, at your service. ✿

Janielle
Angel of Ease

Kari

Angel of Self Love

All Angels function under love, like a big mirror of God, in an exact reflection. Every single aspect of creation is a part of this love. The ability to love starts with self acceptance, then self appreciation growing and moving into self love. As you live through the various parts in the play of life, as a child loving its parents, as parents loving and caring for the child, as partner and team players, and then loving all of life as One, all of these parts are played in greater depth and truth, when once you love and accept yourself. For all is a reflection of self. With love of self, love is returned from all reflecting parties.

Change yourself, within yourself, and all of creation shifts and changes to reflect this back to you. Hence the instructions to attend yourself before others. Make corrections within the self and this will change your relationships with others.

My loving angelic essence of Self Love heals all. Everyone and everything can benefit from more love, acceptance, and appreciation. Open your mind and heart, dear friend, to my loving ministrations for many are the emotional scars upon your being. Invite and allow my assistance in healing old hurts, old barriers to love. I am your Angel of Self Love, come to you to first love thyself. All else follows this one mighty step.

Kari
Angel of
Self Love

Open, dear one, to my loving gift, for I am pure Love. Apply this gift of love in full, generous measure to all you do for best results. Smooth on the salve of love for bruised feeling, bent egos, and unappreciated hearts. I am Kari, your Angel of Self Love, here offering my essence to flavor all you do and all you are.

Open to my loving heart, allow my soothing appreciation, let my glowing radiance uplift your innermost self, the one that hides and cringes in guilt, and sorrow, and loneliness. The one you rejected and abandoned and left for dead, severed and buried as you 'grew up.' Let me cherish this dear part of you back to you, as you lovingly reunite.

You are all as actors in the play of life, and each of you gets to play each part, some more lofty than others, but a star, none the less, in each role. Celebrate your performance. Well done! See how you support one another in your parts in the play, all actors on a stage, dutifully and lovingly playing your parts.

Open your heart to your own dear contributions to life, your gifts to God, your expressions of life with feeling! You are a Star! Accept your applause. Encore! You've done well. Now love yourself for a job well done. I'm right by your side, applauding your effort. What an incredible performance! You so much became the actor that you forgot your true Self.

Awaken now, dear friend, to the loving attention of all your brothers and sisters in this play of life. To act with awareness of Self (the Higher Self clearly and consiously connected to God) and love of self (the lower self only semi-conscious of its connection to God) presents you with the opportunity to share more broadly and richly.

Open to your self worth and self value for these are great in the eyes of God. Open to receive the gift of Love and appreciation for all you are, have been and will be. Feel His gifts bestowed on the breeze blowing through your hair, on the radiant sunlight bathing you in brilliance, as a warm inner glow as His Love ignites your own self acceptance and self love.

My gift, dear friend, is the awakening to the beauty of yourself, the perfection of who you are, the joy of being in Self! With the gift of unconditionally loving the self, you begin to radiate Love like a star. This is now your Being and it pours forth to others in a rich, loving flow.

This is the gift of Love I engender in all who ask and allow my loving attentions. This mighty gift of God I offer in His name. I am lovingly at your service, for all who ask. All of Earth responds to love in kind. Open to accept my gifts of Love. This is the gift that multiples. I am Kari, Angel of Self Love. ✿

Miklenael

Angel of Innovation

W ith the Angels as your team members, innovations pour into awareness at an unprecedented rate. Possibilities abound and innovations emerge within all realms of life as creating and changing become joyful play. The gifts of God offered through these seventy-two Angels, of which I, Miklenael (*mik lin' ay el'*), the Angel of Innovation, am a part, open the doors of ease and flow in creativity as never before in the akashic (universal etheric library) records of Earth.

For instance, with the combined energies of the Angels of Thinking, Diversity, Cooperation, Persistence, Learning and Results, just to name a few of the many transformative energies, results can be beyond all previous conceptions of innovations.

I am your Angel of Innovation present now as your assistant in all matters of innovation, should you ask my assistance. Allow your mind and heart, indeed even your physical body to open and breathe in the energies I offer to see and feel new ways of doing and being, of thinking and creating, of cooperating and manifesting. The possibilities are endless, and now much more available.

I urge you to open to cooperative living, to seek ways of uniting the whole, and caring for the entire ecosystem, which includes humanity. Open to the good and sustenance of the whole, and seek answers and resolution to the growth and evolution of all. These directions are naturally strongly supported now in Earth's ascension times.

Open to new possibilities in life and living, for these are vastly different from your past, and profoundly superior in ease, comfort, and joy, as well as more effective and productive. New times and energies are upon you and all of humanity. I offer assistance in understanding this and utilizing these incredible energies and the knowledge available for those who choose to open to these energies.

I am Miklenael, your Angel of Innovation, available to assist. I await your call. ✿

Miklenael

Angel of Innovation

Placidias

Angel of Patience

Often individuals have an idea of how something 'should be done,' and of course, desire quick completion of the task. Impatience sets in, and you are caught in a treadmill of 'hurry up' energy, focused on some future point, rather than the present. This future focus necessarily robs you of your peace, for you have little control over a a future moment. Your creation abilities are for *present* time.

I am Placidias (*pla sid' ee us'*), your Angel of Patience, and I admonish you to accept my gift of patience, to enjoy the moment, to be present to the joy, the gifts of the moment. By focusing your attention on the *present*, that moment of creation of your reality, you then infuse life into your present reality, with your essence, instead of some possible future reality.

Live in the present and appreciate the moment. The timing is perfect. Be still and appreciate each moment, even in the bursts of daily activity. Allow my ministering energies of patience and feel the peace of God descend upon you. It's like arriving home after a long journey, when first you allow yourself to relax in patience.

Take any energy of impatience and channel it into constructive organizational steps or playful activities, or even work. Be present and honor the timing of each moment, each person with ease and patience.

Be gentle with yourself. As you feel impatience, be still and feel what is really happening. Is your impatience a habit learned from a parent or in school? Is it just your reaction to another's actions, as you see an aspect of yourself you would prefer

Letter. sf
Sketton. Pf
merged. ADD

Placidias
Angel of Patience

to ignore? Do you feel a knot in your stomach, so that anger and irritation radiate from you?

I know how you feel as impatience becomes your reaction to life, and outcomes rarely measure up to your expectations. The growing unhappiness within manifests as impatience as you ignore real causes. Are you numb to the effect of impatience on another as you habitually push another or criticize their way of doing?

My dear friend, allow my help now, to gentle your own soul, to calm the feeling to hurry, to relax the habit of rushing. Call my energies of patience to begin to joyfully appreciate again in each moment.

There's no rush. You create every moment of your reality, so I beg you, please be present. By infusing the moment with your loving attention, you create the best possible outcomes for yourself and all others you touch.

I am here, present now, to share my patient, healing energies in your life. Open to my loving, calming energies and we, you and I together, can create the life you really want. Allow me to soften the brusque exterior that you use to push, as you shield yourself from the inner guidance that is stirring within.

Come back to center. Be still inside. Open to the gentle guidance and clarity that will calm your soul and direct your mind to more productive and fulfilling thoughts and actions. Allow my ministrations to smooth the knots in your stomach, to gentle the grip in your middle, as you again breathe fully and slowly of the moment.

Open your eyes and heart to see others as being the best they can be, in every moment. Concern yourself with your own behavior, and come to acceptance of this first. I know you and others may feel confused, unsure, or unhappy, so that your attention to, and performance of, the task may suffer. The pause you take in these moments may allow your inner guidance system to finally be heard.

Allow your friend or acquaintances, or even that stranger, allow them to move slowly, or be thoughtful, to pause. Allow them to do it their way. Variety, the gloriously different aspects of each and every one of you, is expression of individuality. Most of you value this highly. Appreciate this in your neighbor. Appreciate their creativity, even as you like someone to appreciate your own creations.

Patience, my friend, is a joy to feel, a peacefulness that lets you most efficiently create your desired reality. I am Placidias, your Angel of Patience, at your service. I await your call. ✿

Unuliel

Angel of Protection

P rotection is a two sided gift. Although probably unconscious of it now, you choose your experiences and, in fact, orchestrate and design much of life yourself, whether you be victim or perpetrator. Protection comes into play at that point in evolution where the energies of density attempt to hold the stasis, and when the individual has consciously (to some degree) chosen change. Protection may be a booster to the choice of an individual to change with grace.

Overshielding one from a chosen experience is against this world's prime directive. For it is indeed the experience that allows growth, and subsequent release of old patterns. Our Angelic protection softens the fear, and other strong emotions that may hold one back from embracing an experience in life.

Call on me to strengthen your resolve in your choices. I will assist in your confidence that you can indeed go through this and love again. I am the ever present Guardian Angel. I shield and protect you as you choose. In the choosing of more light and more love, our energies, yours and mine, form a greater shield, more and more impervious to the densities of inertia.

Know that I am always with you in love and service. Pull in and strengthen my energies by *asking* me to help. It is my everlasting joy to assist you now in the time of change and transition to the Light and Love of our One Creator.

My protection is to ensure your progress home to the Heart of God. Choose wisely how you live your life, for my support and protection is indeed complete for the true path homeward. Delays are not brooked now, and a speedy exit may indeed be the straighter path home. So, dear one, call me, that I may be of assistance. My heart is full with love for those who struggle and slip. Ever watchful am I for an opportunity to assist.

I am Unuliel (*oo noo' lee el'*), your Guardian Angel, awaiting your call for assistance. I stand ever ready to shield you from danger, to assist in growth on your path, to lend strength and endurance in your struggle home. I come to you to soften fear of change and growth, to uphold your confidence in your choices, and push you forward when you but ask.

My wings of God's Love and Light enfold you always, with your permission, in all walks of life. I am your Guardian Angel ever ready and ever eager to protect you from harms way. I walk beside you always, if you but ask. I am Unuliel, the Angel of Protection, at your service.

Call me to assist on your journey home to the Heart of God. My wings of Light and Love gently enfold you as I shield you from danger and strengthen your resolve to grow and love. I am ever-present as I await your call. Call me. I am here to help. I am Unuliel, the ever present Guardian Angel. ✿

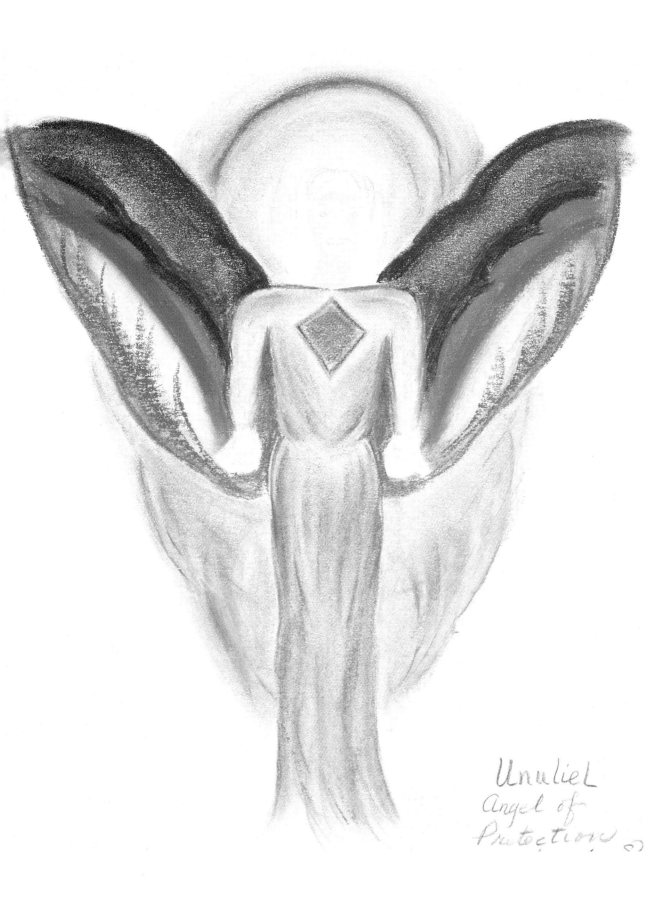

Unuliel
Angel of
Protection

Escielle

Angel of Peace

Always call for peace first in any disturbing situation, and with peace well established, all other creative Light activities can ensue. As peace becomes strong within the individual, situation, or activity, all other aspects of Light gain entrance. Peace precedes happiness, joy, bliss, love, harmony, perfect health, and fullness of Being. It is the gap, the turning point, the moment of utter silence. Peace is the basis of all Light and Love.

Call on me, Escielle (*esh she' el'*), your Angel of Peace, to hold you in times of anguish and sorrow. Allow my peaceful love to envelop and infuse your aching heart or your angry mind. Ask and I will lend a hand to pull you into God's peaceful embrace. This intention can be sent *anywhere in the world* by you who call Me. All is possible from this new starting point.

Ask and I will answer with my peaceful, loving infusion of golden energy. Invite the energies of peace to be a part of your life so you can begin anew. I am Escielle, your Angel of Peace, here to lovingly serve you in times of turmoil and pain. Peace is God's loving, nurturing basis for all life, all activities, for Beingness. I await your call. I am Escielle. ✿

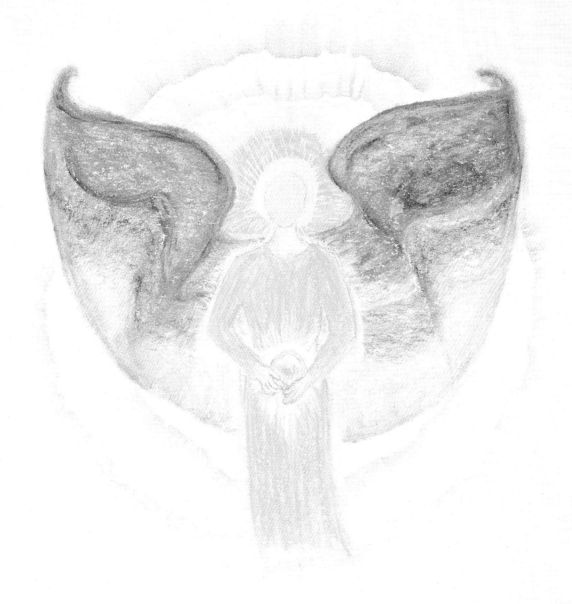

Escielle,
Angel of Peace

Mericu

Angel of Serenity

I n serenity you are centered and whole within the midst of activity, living the connection with God, with inner and outer calm. I am Mericu, *(meh' ra koo')*, your Angel of Serenity, fully available to assist you in creating and maintaining serenity in life. My energies are an aspect of silence in activity, a peaceful knowingness in the maturity of your spirit.

Open your heart and mind in trust and reconnection to God, Oneness with God as your stabilizer, and stand in your light of serenity. With this divine reference, feel centered and whole within the midst of activity, fully active and yet still, silent and connected within. Open to this fullness of you within, living your truth, clear and sure inside, soft and compassionate, living life fully from a quiet center of Oneness with God.

Open to a life of serenity, the serene life of joy and bliss that flow gently inward and outward in a celebration of life. Serenity keeps the door of communication with God continuously open. Divine guidance and intervention are a natural part of life in serenity. Wholeness is the norm with clear awareness, good health, and life in *sync* and balance.

Invite serenity into your life. Open to your own centeredness, your own inner cohabitation with God. Breathe fully of this Oneness, asking for more conscious

Mericu
Angel of Serenity

union within.   I, Mericu, your Angel of Serenity, engender this openness, this connection and experience of the quiet center of life within.

Invite my help and I will gently assist you in moving into serenity, creating this quiet stability within and without. Serenity is your heritage, your right. Just ask for it, then allow and expect it, knowing you, too, can be serene in life.

I am Mericu, your Angel of Serenity. Call on my assistance for life in serenity. Invite my energies as you proceed through your active life of turmoil and change, for serenity can buoy your energies and balance your emotions. I gladly open my heart to your needs and offer my assistance when called. I invite your call. ✿

Jemlien

Angel of Grace

I am Jemlien (*Jem len*), your Angel of Grace, gifting you with the ability to shift and change your realities in a moment with the use of grace. My loving essence of grace is like *magic dust*, for all can ascend above restraints and create new realities with grace as you relax and become the graceful flow. My gifts to you allow situations, beliefs, values, all aspects to improve regardless of previous limitations.

This gift of God is active on Earth now, if you allow and invite it. I offer my assistance to skillfully apply grace and change your world. Open your heart to the vast possibilities before you. All is possible. Work with me, your Angel of Grace to apply the added energies of grace to comfortably speed your changes and exquisitely enhance the outcomes.

Eagerly I fly to your request, assisting in graceful changes, graceful growth, ever so gentle and yet miraculously superior in results. I am your simple, added ingredient for a life of ease and grace, with profound results. I temper my essence, tailoring my energies to you, the receiver, depending on the desired degree of change.

Examine your life now. Any desire for change in any aspect? Want to change anything? I am as a fairy Godmother (father), with a magic wand, activating the life force within you to create changes that support your growth. Your wishes are unlimited, though you will soon draw your transformative strength from your own life force without my help.

Life can be easy, fun, and magical. One grace-filled person, moving about and living life on Earth, can share this essence of grace with thousands of others, creating a wake of magical moments and miraculous changes. Invite my assistance to get started on the path of grace. Everyone is eligible, all are included. Accept my grace and I will engender yours. I am Jemlien, your Angel of Grace. ✿

Jemlien
Angel of
Grace

E A Terry 9/9_

Derilicium

Angel of Resonance

I am Derilicium (*de ruh lee' see um*), your Angel of Resonance, here to offer you knowledge and assistance in resonance. As few of you have thought of this concept, and less of you are concerned with this today, I first offer my knowledge of resonance.

Resonance is the resultant shift in frequencies, the shift in vibration to an equilibrium point within a group. Tuning forks begin to vibrate when another nearby is vibrating. This is an example of resonance.

Each human has a certain frequency, vibrates at a certain rate within his body. This rate is increasing, even as Earth's frequency is increasing steadily now. With your own changes in frequency, you will feel like you are changing, and know that shifts are occurring within. You will also feel the changes in those around you, and need to know how to regulate your frequency to maintain your space and your comfort. Holding your own resonance consistently rather than lowering it to meet another, to interact or share with another, becomes a necessity now.

This centeredness of holding to who you are, regardless of where you are and who you are with, is holding your resonance. This ability is necessary to feel and live your own truth today. Holding resonance allows you to make free will choices, in

Devilicium
Angel of
Resonance

your own truth, and not another's. This allows you the freedom to know your preferences, choose for yourself, and act accordingly.

With the clarity of resonance, you have the choice of what resonance you move toward, as in a guide or friend with a higher frequency. For a teacher who has achieved a higher frequency with the accompanying abilities that manifest with these higher frequencies, it will be important to know how to share that experience of higher frequency without lowering it, or lowering it to meet the student and then showing how to raise it, giving that experience of higher frequency.

An effective teacher shares the knowledge of the actual experience of the higher frequency and the emotions that accompany this experience. This teacher knows how to lower his frequency to the student's level, then increases his frequency again, thus leading the student to raise his own frequency.

Saints and gurus, those known for their higher frequencies, are able to steadily hold their high frequency, producing *darshan*, where those in proximity begin to resonate to this higher frequency. Darshan is the gift of sharing the essence of being through resonance.

Your being today, right now, affects another, and this another, rippling outward and inward. I thank you, dear one, for allowing my energies to be a part of your being today. My assistance helps you firmly hold your frequency amid adversity and in the thick of life, remaining and increasingly connected to God within as your reference.

Invite my help to feel more comfortable and sure in daily life, as you grow and change. You will feel more vulnerable in times of change, which you will find is *most* of the time now. My assistance helps you stay centered and clearly in touch with the desired direction and steps to achieve these change.

Invite my assistance to hold your resonance clearly and boldly, as you shift and change in this ascending world. In the past you lowered your frequency to meet the challenges and to survive, seemingly disconnecting from God and your guides. I say to you this is no longer necessary. Invite my assistance to help hold your resonance and remain consciously connected to God and your guides now in these changes.

I am your stabilizer in these times of change. Ask and I assuredly will assist. It is my joy to assist. I await your call. Blessings on you now in these times of great transition. I am Derilicium. ✿

Haboine

Angel of Benevolence

J am Haboine (*hah' boy nay'*) your Angel of Benevolence, sharing love, good wishes, expectancy, enthusiasm, and resonance. Long have I overshadowed many of you as you felt to assist another, and stepped forward with an outstretched hand. I share my benevolent energies of giving and helping others, my energies always balanced with wisdom.

Know that I am present whenever hospitality is offered, and when arms are opened to comfort and welcome. I am here and ready to help whenever called. I will assist in creating situations where sharing and helping help others will help them to learn about sharing this same gift with others.

Often an individual creates a situation to learn and complete a lesson, never to have a need to repeat this pattern again. This lesson may seem harsh and cruel, and yet this individual needs exactly what he has created, for had he been able to complete the lesson with lesser situations, he would have done that. My loving, caring energies often are just supportive as an individual goes through 'his stuff.'

Call me, Haboine, into your life when you desire more benevolence at home, work, or play with family, friends or strangers. I am as an arm of God helping to make things happen comfortably. Whether you are asking for help from God, or want to be the arm of God, I gladly share my benevolent arms with you in assistance. Open your heart and arms to receive the sustenance of God, to feel and know that all is provided within your divine plan. Ever watchful and helpful, I come on a whisper of a wish, a faint hope for assistance. Allow this gift of God to flow into your life, accepting abundance in gratitude and love.

Great are the gifts I bring, with your request and acceptance. And greatest of these is the knowingness of abundance; that in this awareness, you turn to another to share and care. This indeed is part of the flow of abundance and plenty from and to God.

In God's love and abundance, I am Haboine, your Angel of Benevolence, at your service. ✿

Haboine
Angel of
Benevolence
EA Jerry ♥

Gilandriel

Angel of Courage

ourage is not just for the warrior, but for you who are willing and brave enough to look at yourself, and *see* and acknowledge yourself as the creator of your life.

You are who, where, and what you are because you intended it and manifested it. Often a more *macro* view is necessary to pull this into focus, but courage is needed to acknowledge this creation and admit that it may need change and maintenance on many levels, that it is indeed a dynamic system. What worked in childhood frequently will not work in adolescence or adulthood. The first lessons you learned and applied to get what you desired may well be ineffective to the point of getting the opposite of what you want today.

It takes courage to examine yourself and all of your motives, desires, aspirations, the full inner workings of your being, and unravel and discard those tried and previously productive programs. These old programs, deeply embedded very early in your life, are largely emotionally driven and are intertwined with the very basic needs of security, survival, hope, love, and sustenance.

It takes courage to go back and feel those moments when these tapes started and discard them, to choose an alternate behavior more appropriate for now. You have to be brave to examine yourself and admit fault or cause, to let down your armor, and be

Silendriel
Angel of Courage

vulnerable as you shift, change, and choose different ways of interacting with and relating to your world. Can you let yourself feel how you may have hurt others as you chose and acted? Can you acknowledge to yourself the great pain and sorrow that you buried deep inside, that just will not stay stuffed any longer?

It takes courage to be vulnerable and honest with yourself, to *really* see yourself as you see others, or project and see yourself in others. It takes courage to *own* your creation of life, and accepting that, choose to change and grow.

Tantrums are expressed anger about unattained outcomes. Spilt milk. It's history. Be present and real. Brutally honest. This takes courage, but it is also an incredible injection of life, totally invigorating, completely reconnecting you back to life, like a breath of fresh air filling your lungs to full capacity.

I am your Angel of Courage, Gilandriel (*gih lahn' dree el'*), here to offer my help in living life fully, embracing truth and change while staying connected to your God center. Whether warrior or servant, whether artisan or teacher, courage is for all of you who are brave enough to take responsibility for what you have created and consider that *you* may have to change to create a more desirable life.

I bring you courage to add to your own energies. I bring the added *umph!* to realize sooner that understanding and deliberate choice can make a world of difference in your life and many others' lives. I bring you strength to stand up against the pressures to stay in the old patterns. Accept my gifts of strength to see and accept your creational role in life, and to know that you can make a change for the better. I bring the courage to grow wise, to open to new ways, to believe in miracles and a better life.

Invite my gift and I will shower you with the strength to accept the gifts of opportunity, to see the opportunity in every moment. I will strengthen your resolve to stay present, to use each first window of opportunity, to pick up the pieces of your life right where you are now and begin to remold and recreate from that point forward. Regardless of your walk in life, my energies are useful and powerful. I am at your service, Gilandriel, your Angel of Courage. I await your call. ✿

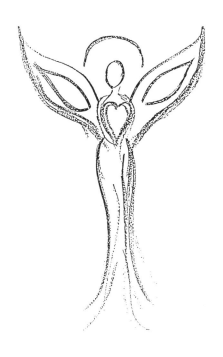

It takes courage to own your creation of life, and accepting that, choose to change and grow . . .

~*Angel Gilandriel.*

Segment Four

13 Angels

Angel of Vision, Mulok
Angel of Joy, Anziliel
Angel of Happiness, Angelica
     Morning Star
Angel of Child's Love, Vehleju
Angel of Manifesting, Maneziel
Angel of Pleasure, Gloriel
Angel of Now, Ohilo
Angel of Miracles, Eldriek
Angel of Endurance, Duronelle
Angel of Enthusiasm, Ethulael
Angel of Learning, Gilane
Angel of Results, Celukel
Angel of Persistence, Lolijael

Mulok

Angel of Vision

pen to your God given abilities to *see your reality in totality*. This more than anything else will allow and encourage the full ability of your vision to manifest. Many of you have chosen to shift your visual ability so you see life selectively, so you don't see what you choose to avoid. You may have then added further visual adjustments with glasses.

As you open to accept your creations in life, and to recreate and change this by choice, your vision will change and improve. Allow me, Mulok (*moo lok'*), your Angel of Vision, to assist you in seeing your creations fully. This is a first and necessary step toward the development of your higher visual abilities. Other Angels are available to assist you in changing these realities in multifarious ways.

The time approaches now when more individuals will open to their long dormant innate abilities. I am here, your Angel of Vision, to help you see your reality in totality, including the greater, broader reality, beyond what has been possible with your two physical eyes. These eyes have served humanity well during your period of deep sleep, but now, as you awaken to who you really are, your full capabilities will begin to blossom, with a little encouragement.

Allow me, your Angel of Vision, to assist in opening your inner eye to see the realities as we, the Angels, see them. The development of this inner vision opens

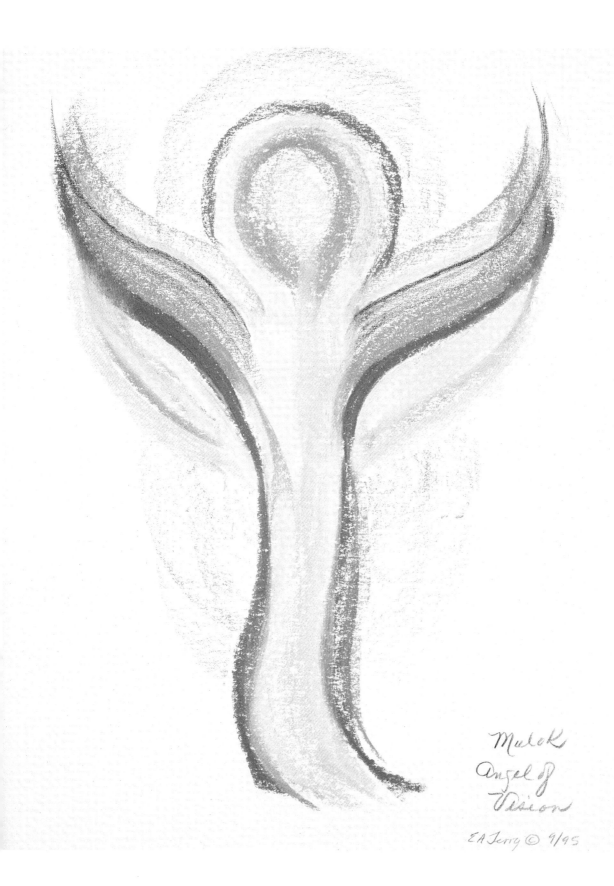

Mulek
Angel of
Vision

EA Terry © 9/95

many new possibilities for you. It allows you to see at distances, and to communicate more fully and easily. Telepathy, communicating with another, as if you were there present, uses this inner vision. It eventually includes the senses of touch, smell, taste and hearing as your telepathic abilities mature.

Attend to the healing and balancing of your aura, your emotional body, as inner peace and fullness of breath support this growth of vision. I am your Angel of Vision, here present to help you adjust and shift, growing in your ability to use God's gifts of Light through your third eye. This inner vision helps you clearly see the inner and outer beauty of an individual, regardless of their station in life or physical appearance, as the aura of an individual becomes apparent. One with this open and functioning higher perception system soon learns to correlate aura information to the truth of the individual.

Your visual abilities will grow to allow appreciation of finer levels of creation. 'Visioning' is part of your creation process, for attention to detail helps you create with more exactness. Open to my ministering energies and ask that I assist you in your process of bringing this inner vision to full capacity. Gently will I assist you in aligning and balancing, slowly testing and checking as you grow in your abilities to visualize, focus and perceive. I am Mulok. I await your call. ✿

Anziliel

Angel of Joy

I am Anziliel (*an zee' lee el'*), the Angel of Joy, ever joyfilled and happy, spreading bliss at every opportunity, and even creating some of those opportunities. Even as we are joyous over the Earth changes and spiritual growth of many on Earth, we rejoice with you in this moment. As you open your heart to the gifts of joy I bestow on you, all of creation rejoices with you. This is the joy of the One Creator reflected to you and back to Him. The resonance of this joy builds in strength, creating joyous, heart expanding hymns of bliss, the music of the universe.

My joyless One, come into my arms, feel my loving embrace and my gift of joy in your heart. Come to me, oh heavy of heart: let my joy infect you now. Long has humanity lived a joyless existence. *No more!* Joy in life, in being, is my gift. Just ask!

I am eager to burst with joy in your life, in your work, in your family, and within your heart. Know now that life in joy is my gift and your heritage, if you but allow my joyful loving energies to merge with you, spread through your being and into your environment. Invoke my energies, my loving joyfulness and feel the warmth flow through your being. Feel the glow of joy as I infuse your life with everlasting joy in the moment.

Expect the miracle of joy now as I, Anziliel, enfold you in my wings of purest joy and loving bliss. Call on me Anziliel, the Angel of Joy, to lift your spirits, to soar with the Angels. It is my greatest joy to bring a smile to your face, a lift to your heavy heart, and a hug to your weary soul. Only ask and my joy will gush through your life in wave upon wave of pure unabashed joy and love. You are my joy as you ask. I am Anziliel and I am at your service in joyful expectancy. Joy to the World! ✿

Anziliel
Angel of Joy

Angelica Morning Star

Angel of Happiness

T he full prosperity of God's Love creates unshakable happiness. God's Love enters and anchors in your heart. Only this brings true and lasting happiness. This joy filled, blissful feeling is as an opening of the heart chakra to full bloom with a radiant flow of energy *into* the center and emerging *from* this center simultaneously.

Happiness is always a feeling within and cannot be created from without. No thing will bring happiness, will 'fix it' for you. All of your striving for material goods is but a veil, a smoke screen to the action needed to create happiness. And yet many, nay, most on Earth strive to amass goods, get things in search of happiness, only to arrive at that empty place of no joy, and even greater unhappiness.

Call me, Angelica Morning Star, your Angel of Happiness, when that emptiness sets in, when you achieve your goals and yet are empty of the happiness of union with God. For no thing of the world will produce happiness without the love of God as part of it. Call me anytime to infuse your life with meaning again, to expand your heart in love and happiness, to assist you in knowing the true feeling of happiness, and how to maintain this greatest of pleasures.

I am Angelica Morning Star, lovingly at your service. Your happiness is ever my happiness as we cocreate the moments of your life in union with God. ✿

Angelica Morning Star
Angel of Happiness

Vehleju

Angel of Child's Love

I am your Angel of Child's Love, Vehleju *(veh leh joo')*, and I offer assistance in remembering and being the unconditional loving Being you are and were as you entered this realm of Earth. Feel the soft, gentle open heart of the child of God within. Feel the joyful delight of the child's heart with all of creation, totally accepting and reveling in the splendor and beauty, the dance of creation. A child's heart is fully open and giving, completely loving and accepting. Remember the joy of an open heart, flowing in the delight of love, One with all of creation.

"A totally vulnerable place?" you ask. Yes, and I say to you, it's the only place to be! Allow yourself to re-experience the joy of the child's love, the child within you. Open your heart to the love within, the simple, innocent, unconditional love of a child. Feel this innocent love radiate from your heart, from your being. Breathe deeply of the flow of this healing, blissful love. Remember the time when trust had never been an issue. Remember the joy of life in unconditional love, as this reawakens in your heart and radiates from your being.

A child's love, simple and innocent, full of trust and hope and joy in life, allows the ego to rest, to relax and allow reconnection to God via your Higher Self. This love is your anchor point to God. God is anchored into your heart deep within the innocence of this inner child that is you. This love is within every human, all of humanity.

138

Vehleju
Angel of Child's Love

Open to the child's love within your heart and allow the healing balm of innocent love to bathe your being and heal your soul. I, Vehleju, the Angel of Child's Love, offer you this healing balm of love, which is already your own. Open to your connection to God within and allow your own innocent love to radiate to Him. I only facilitate you allowing and accepting this gift of Love. Invite my help and I loving share my gifts of assistance with you. I am Vehleju. ✿

Maneziel

Angel of Manifesting

I, the Angel of Manifesting, offer you assistance to *make it happen*. Dedicated to the process of clearly and thoroughly manifesting on the causal plane and then pulling the creation through to this plane quickly and perfectly, I work in those areas of your mind that often elude your conscious thinking. You feel the answer is just around the corner, as you mull over a problem and seek the solution.

Call me, Maneziel (*ma nee' zee el'*) , the Angel of Manifesting, when an added boost and new perspective are needed. Ask me to pull it over into your conscious mind, which actually means that I will assist in broadening your awareness enough to perceive our work together. Then your conscious participation and intentions can be much more effective in manifesting in a more three dimensional way. 'Imaging-in,' imagination is a very powerful tool in creating. It's the only way Angels work, by intentions. Join the Angels and ascend to your true image; begin to use your own body and mind in the way God intended.

Create intentionally, consciously. Ask for guidance and assistance from me, Maneziel, your Angel of Manifesting. Let me assist you in far grander and more perfect creations than you could alone--initially, that is. It is my intention that you learn how to create like the Angels. It is just a remembering process. Ask for my help to awaken your memories of creating with thought and love. I can help you remember your own expansion in the heart, filled with intimate love and appreciation as you imaged in creations. Love is a core ingredient of all creations. The Love energy is the seed from which to build and expand through every cell of your creation. The Love energy instills your creation with far greater perfection, its very image being transformative to the viewer.

Call on me, Maneziel, your Angel of Manifesting. Great and beautiful can our creations be. My assistance is freely given for all creations bringing greater alignment, balance, and growth to humanity.

Ask in your heart, "Is this creation that I now desire the best I can image, uplifting and beneficial to humankind? Will this creation have an enlivening, enlightening effect on its users?" If the answers to these questions are yes, call me, for I will freely and joyfully assist you in speedily and gloriously accomplishing your goal.

Know that, at your request and with your permission, I may assist you with improvements in the object of your focus, even as you 'see' how to create it. I am Maneziel, your Angel of Manifesting. Ask, call me, and I can be with you daily, energizing your creation process in every moment; indeed, your reality is literally your own creation. I ask to assist you to open your knowingness and acceptance of this process in which you have participated, by default in large part, until now. Open your awareness to your part in the creation of your life as it has been and is now. Know you chose this and created it, shaped it by belief patterns and personal values, by accepting reality as rigid.

Are some of you in a rut, on a treadmill of life? Stuck? Unhappy? Angry, vengeful? Sad, unhealthy, broke? Desperate? I am here, now present, to help you manifest in a conscious, loving manner, and to open your awareness to your unknowing part in this process in the past. Ask and I will help you remember, help you know you can change life by creating consciously and joyfully.

Whatever your present situation, if you are ready for a change, call me. I'll happily assist you in creating an outstanding solution. My joy, my pleasure is your call to me. My services are endless and joyful, your risk nil. You have every thing to gain by calling, far more than you may imagine. I await your call. I am Maneziel, at your service. ✿

Manesiel
Angel of Manifesting

Gloriel

Angel of Pleasure

All know pleasure and desire more of it. This is a human trait even as it is an Angelic trait, and not to be denied. Yes, *pleasure*, this being different from joy, and more easily understood and felt by most of you at this time. I am Gloriel (*glo ree el'*), your Angel of Pleasure, here to offer my assistance in creating pleasure in all that you are and that you create in your life here and now.

My energies infuse pleasure into the moment, bringing this fullness to each experience. Those in the thralls of addiction are encouraged to call on my loving ministrations to assist in replacing these destruction tendencies with loving, joyful, and healthful pleasures of the body, mind, heart and soul.

Call on me to be with you at all times as change will ever increase in these times of growth. I am ever at your service to glow and infuse you with the golden energy of pleasure in each moment. Never again will the hunger for pleasures and comforts of the body rule your life, as you invoke my name and energies to merge with you and assist you on your journey home.

Even as you call me, feel the rain of golden life force energy infuse your being. Feel your soul and body as one with the pleasure of life and Divinity as One. This, my golden gift of Light and Love to you, will seep into your being, slowly opening the doors that lock out your pleasure in life. Many memories and teachings have taught

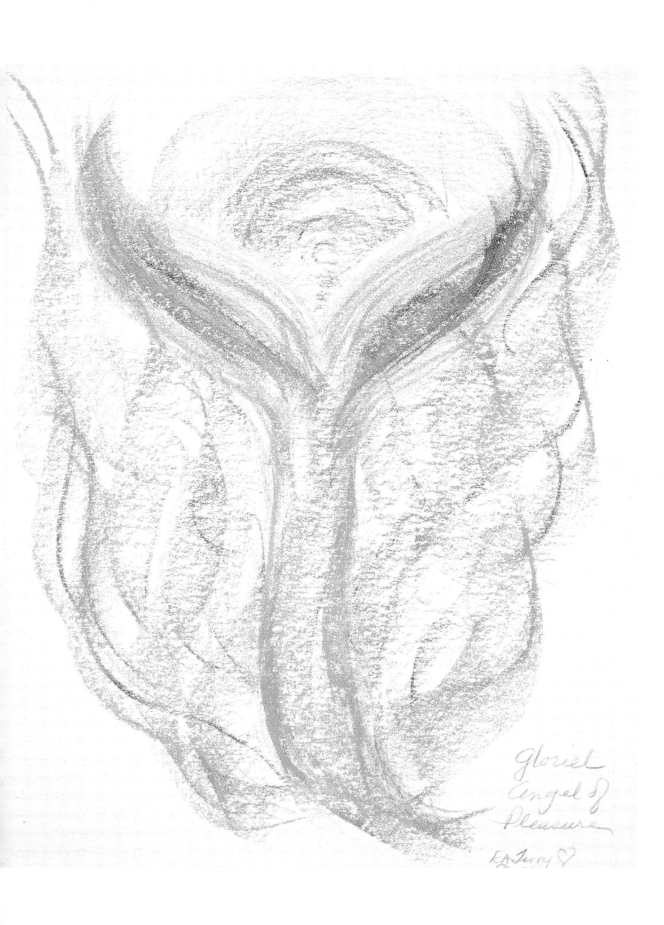

Gloriel
Angel of
Pleasure

K A Terry ♡

you that pleasure is sinful and to be avoided for salvation. Know that pleasure is your God given heritage and an essential aspect of your experience here on Earth. Pleasure can be constructive and uplifting even as it helps you to grow in love and appreciation of others and yourself.

Open once again to trust that God has not led you astray, and that you have found your answer to the compelling needs and desires of your life. Feel my gift of warmth infusing your being and lighting your awareness, enfolding your opening heart as you turn to and accept this glorious gift of God. Trust again that your needs will be met fully, that your need for pleasure in life is only the door to other great mysteries unfolding before you.

I am your Angel of Pleasure, infusing you with a golden warmth, even as you call for me. Invite my assistance, and begin to enjoy life more fully, each and every moment. I await your call. I am Gloriel, your Angel of Pleasure. ✿

Ohilo

Angel of Now

I, Ohilo (*oh hie' loh'*), the Angel of Now, am ready to jump into your arms *NOW!* I offer the gift of being fully present, in the present moment, living this moment fully. While planning for the future and learning from the past are useful, these two can also be traps that magnetize your attention to such a degree that you are rarely present and, therefore, only partially effective at being and living.

With all attention and energies fully present, fully aware in the moment, your abilities expand and your reality becomes more vibrant. This very attention, this vision, allows you to create in the moment. You do, indeed, create your reality in each moment, whether by clear intention or tacit default. While being fully present and stable in your awareness of the moment, you *can* also expand your awareness into the greater fullness of realities that are adjacent to your immediate knowingness.

Guilt and worry dissipate as you become fully present, involved in your present state of affairs. Guilt focuses on historical events, as you sorrow over less than desired outcomes, feeling 'responsible.' You become fully responsible when you live in the moment, making the best of each moment, from the *present* time on.

Worry focuses on future events taking your energies forward, pulling you out of the present. The treadmill of worry robs you of your present creative energies, which

147

would in turn create the more desirable future, that would alleviate the need to worry. A catch-22 situation.

You have little control over past and future, but full control of the present. At the moment you may be running on automatic. Try shifting your awareness totally to the present each time you become aware of being less than present. Time indeed 'goes by' anyway, so why not create the best you know to create in each moment. As these 'best creations' multiply, and being present becomes your way of living, you will notice that the past and future take care of themselves.

Being fully present, creating, living the best you know implies accessing 'first windows.' This is full awareness of opportunities as they present themselves the first time around, with clear awareness of accepted responsibilities and required actions with quick resolutions. This does not mean worrying about all the various ramifications of chosen or possible actions, but choosing intentionally your direction and creation, and doing it. *Just do it!*

Your times and frequencies on Earth now are active with the principles of resonance and grace, to create magically immediate results from desires, vision, and action. Choose and use your energies well, for when you do, they are powerful beyond belief.

I am Ohilo, your Angel of Now, present and available to assist you in becoming fully present. In the moment that you call, already I am with you. ✿

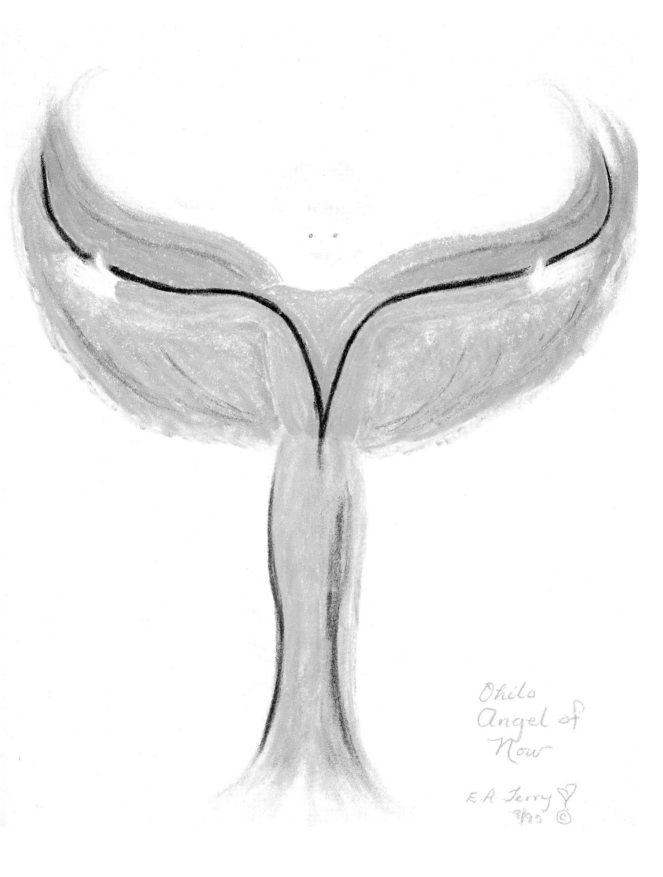

Ohilo
Angel of
Now

E.A Terry
9/95 ©

Eldriek

Angel of Miracles

J am Eldriek (*el drik'*), the Angel of Miracles, here to energize requests to the Angels. Miracles are held by humanity to be impossibilities that 'come true,' outcomes far beyond currently held belief systems. I am ready and waiting to cocreate a miracle with you. Ask in reverence and expectancy, with gratitude for the outcome; for by believing, you cause it to be. Allow me to boost your belief in yourself and expand the depths of your possibilities. Miracles do happen. Call one to you. Ask for my help with gratitude and expectancy and you open the doors to grand phenomena.

This Earth will become a world of miracles as you open your heart and mind to the angelic offer of communion and cocreation. Help us make miracles an everyday occurrence. Help us change your understanding of miracles--who gets them, when they can happen, why they occur, and the magnitude of these, our cocreated gifts together.

Do you need a miracle now to pay the rent this month? Would it take a miracle to keep your marriage together? Would it take a miracle for you, your child, or friend to change your destructive personal habits to healthy inclinations? Ask for my assistance and we can work miracles together.

Eldriek
Angel of Miracles

Often you will find an outcome creatively different from what you supposed the answer would be. Our angelic vision has a broader scope with greater potential at our disposal. We're a team. Let's work together. Know that your request is heard when you call, and by calling, you become my partner in the miracle we create, cocreators sharing Light and Love.

My specialty is creating miracles. With your help, your openness, your understanding, miracles can happen for everyone everyday. Life can be easy, beautiful. You can feel good again, enthusiastic and happy as you look forward to the joy of the day. You can change your life and do all the things you've been postponing for 'some day soon.' Joy inside, now in this moment, may be your miracle. Or a wish for joy and peace for another.

Ask for my help, for yourself or another in greater need. It is my pleasure to double the joy of miracle making with you. Your request is my miracle and my great joy.

Call me when in need. Then visualize together with me the situation needing change, or the person needing help. Request my assistance and input for resolution. Send your gratitude to God as if it's a 'done deal,' already complete as you release all to God. Your expectancy helps to create your desired outcome and is a magnet to pull it into manifestation. This help from you will greatly assist in bringing forth our miracle.

Miracles come in many ways. As you perceive a need for change in a situation, as you mull around different possibilities in your mind, if you but ask my help, I may pop the answer right into your mind. Many individuals now, awakening to greater realities in life, may come to your aid, just as you recognize your need.

Open to the need for change. See the areas of greater possibilities within yourself and without in your environment, with friends, family, society, your life work. Once you open to possibility of changes, I am ready and available to boost your own energies to create miracles of change. Open your eyes and ears, your awareness and alertness. Open to new energies of enthusiasm and excitement in a whole new way of living and being.

Want a miracle? Ask for it and take part in its creation. This is an open invitation to cocreate Heaven on Earth! Let's do it! Long have I awaited your call to again create miracles together. I breathe a great sigh of relief that we once again join energies in joyous creating.

In Love and Service, I am Eldriek, your Angel of Miracles. ✿

Duronelle

Angel of Endurance

I, Duronelle (*du ron el'*), the Angel of Endurance, bless you now with my ever ready energies to help you keep going, to enliven your will and enthusiasm for life when life seems bleak and dull. I lend strength and guidance to the weary of heart, opening new awarenesses of alternative actions to lighten the load and satisfy the soul. Allow my assistance now in continuing life, holding your resolve firm, and forging ahead in supportive growth patterns. I am here to support and hold you as new insights seep in and root in fertile ground, grow and flower into new directions and accomplishments.

I feel the struggle of all who strive to continue, all who falter and stretch. I know your pain as you reach beyond your limits. Allow my loving ministrations to uplift and energize your reach, your enthusiasm, your will to complete your chosen task with satisfaction and joy. My energies boost your strength and prolong your clarity, as you finish your chosen direction and move on to greater heights and more fulfilling activities. My added energies can hold the still moment in time to re-evaluate and move, change direction and intention, open to more life supporting endeavors.

Invite my energies to assist you, all who strive and struggle, all who feel frozen in time, all who desire change and growth, or even just continued movement. My sustenance of your energies allows you to open your awareness to the greater picture, even as you maintain your *status quo*. This opened awareness lets you see many more possibilities and directions. My added energies help you finish a task more quickly, so you can 'get on with it.' Choose your 'it' consciously. Choose and use my energies with yours to propel yourself forward into superlative horizons.

I am your Angel of Endurance ready and able to assist you. Call and I will answer with gentle yet strong, supporting energies. I am Duronelle, at your service. ✿

Dunomelle

Angel of Endurance

P.C.Poe

Ethulael

Angel of Enthusiasm

I am your Angel of Enthusiasm here today to assist you, and all others whom you touch, in living enthusiastically and joyfully, imbibing each moment of life with vibrant enthusiasm. I eagerly offer you my gushing energies of joyful eagerness in all you do. Just call and I am already with you infusing you with energetic life force, boosting your energy to create and flow into the higher frequencies of being and creating.

Thoughts create. As attention is withdrawn from a creation, it begins to 'dis-create' or crumble, as a house no longer lived in begins to deteriorate. Enthusiasm as emotional energy catalyzes and fertilizes creational thought. It is like gas for the motor of desire. Enthusiasm actually pushes open the thinking pathways of the brain, adding additional capacity to the hardware for thinking and creating. It helps open chakras to flow your life force energies, enlivening you and energizing your physical body into action.

While enthusiasm is a feeling of excitement and exuberance, it is also an attitude of optimism and commitment to a project or activity. It is indicative of belief in life and in attainable, predictable outcomes.

Enthusiasm soars with dependable team members, all equally enthusiastic and aligned toward an intended creation. This combined excitation synergistically excites

Ethulael
Angel of Enthusiasm

P.E. Poe

the fabric of creation into splendid arrays of manifestation. Each creation can have infinite outcomes. With my assistance, just an additional ingredient to add to your energies, one that creates joy and bliss in every activity, you can create more refined, more energized, and more vibrant creations. Just call me and my energies are already a part of you, as your energies flow into everything you do.

Allow my energies to infuse your being, especially when you are low on enthusiasm and less creative thought forms and behavior patterns are directing your attention. Invite my energies to transform your inner space to enthusiastic joy in your present activity. This is my enthusiastic gift. I am Ethulael (*ee thoo' lay el'*) your Angel of Enthusiasm, eagerly awaiting your call. ✿

Gilane

Angel of Learning

earest soul, thank you for asking and receiving me today, for all on Earth have chosen great lessons to complete at this time. I am Gilane (*gi lane'*), your Angel of Learning. The Earth is changing very quickly now, and so all of humanity will, of necessity, need to change and become more fluid in these changes to maintain comfort and joy.

Learning starts with receptivity, openness to acknowledging that your present stance in life may not be serving you well and, in fact, may be sabotaging all that you hold dear. Learning starts with open-mindedly and open-heartedly turning to receive the gifts of growth, change, and insight into your personal beliefs, concepts, and operating programs.

You are indeed a student of school house Earth, and all of this *is* testable material. While there are no wrong choices, you may take the scenic route or a more direct route. Now with accelerating and resetting time, the more direct way may be the route of choice. Even that pathway will be rich in scenarios of growth, largely choreographed and directed by you, under your Higher Self's guidance.

Look to each situation to garner the lesson, to understand why *you* have set this into play. *You* created this moment and this situation to learn about an important aspect of your life. Open to the recurrent patterns in your life and recognize the programs that run them. Go back to the source of these patterns, to the scene that set them running. Use the talking cure, or writing to defuse them. Make a conscious choice now in this clear moment to rewrite the program, to choose a different mode of behavior more aligned with your truth and desired outcome.

Allow, accept, and appreciate the joy of life, the gifts of love and caring, *and* all who participated. There is no blame. You do everything you do by your own choice. You are the divine orchestrator of your life. Each player in your scenarios agreed to play their part. How much some being must love you to play the 'shit' roles you hand out to them, for them to 'do' to you for your learning experience? It could only be one with a deep and abiding love, who understood your needs and desires to resolve a 'hard' and resistant lesson, and so could agree to assist in those roles.

Allowing, accepting, and appreciating these people and all of their baggage lets you see the *macro view* and learn your lesson, by stepping out of the emotional triggers that ensnare you over and over. Step out of the role, out of the game by totally defusing the trigger at its source. This is participation in life at its fullest, making conscious choices in life, rather than defaulting through life and resenting it (life) pushing you around.

You can enjoy the ride and appreciate the process if you choose. I, Gilane, Angel of Learning, offer my assistance freely and gladly to boost your flexibility and fluidity, your understanding and comprehension, your loving and caring. I bring you an openness to new knowledge, an affinity for integrating and applying this new knowledge, and new ways, new energies to flow with the changes, growth, and diversity. My assistance will help you integrate all that is offered by the Angels. I await your call. I am Gilane. ✿

Gilane
Angel of Learning

Celukel

Angel of Results

R esults are all around you. You get results all the time. You are living the results of previous and present choices. Humanity is a race of creators and is living the results of choices. Why not openly and consciously acknowledge this and accept the responsibility for the present, along with the ability to create a different reality, if this one is not what you want?

You often sit in judgment of others, complaining when this, your own reflection, is unacceptable to you. There is no one to blame. All that you have and are, you created. This moment and who you are is a result of previous choices, specific orchestrations of your lives, all to learn and grow.

I am Celukel (*see loo kel'*), your Angel of Results, available to assist in results. This includes recognizing and acknowledging your present results and your creatorhood, and the ability to create consciously and coherently, in accord with your own and God's plan for your life. Your desires lead you to choices and the required action to manifest results.

The required action frequently involves healing, releasing buried emotions, and removing blocks and barriers within you that prevent the flow of energies required for the manifestion of chosen results. I especially assist in these areas of healing, growing, and changing to achieve the desired results. All of life is change and

Celukel
Angel of Results

growth, movement toward God. Results manifest more easily as you release control and allow the movement and shifting of energies through the inner dense areas where you have stored your issues and unresolved lessons.

I offer divine intervention and it is your own, with a little tweaking, some delicate adjustment of your God given energies of creation. I am God's messenger to awaken you to your own creatorhood, to assist you in acknowledging your present creations, and your abilities to create consciously with full awareness of chosen and created results.

I am Celukel, Angel of Results, available to assist you, if this is your choice. The gifts of consciously chosen results are many, as you open to the divine design of creating on Earth. The choice is yours, as are the results. I am at your service for Divine cocreation. ✿

Lolijael

Angel of Persistence

I am Lolijael (*low lee' jay el'*), your Angel of Persistence, and I open my arms and wings to enfold you in my energizing support. Your hardest lessons often bring your greatest returns, and yet many of you falter right on the cusp of completion, never to know the very next step would have been the finish line on that lesson. Often your temper or your weaknesses trip you. Your enthusiasm diminishes and clear vision fogs before you gain the gift of the lesson. You may find yourselves muddled in a mire of difficulties, unsure of your direction and purpose.

Call on me, your Angel of Persistence, to help you maintain clear energies to complete your chosen tasks. Let me help you keep going with an open full heart, clear precise purpose, and healthy energetic body. Let me help you maintain your enthusiasm and joy throughout your tasks, with the Love and Light of God permeating your being and infusing your tasks and outcomes.

You are not alone on this team. Let's play ball. Open your awareness to my energizing strength and joy filled light. With your permission I can assist you at all times, as your strength of body, clarity of mind and love in your heart grow to be constant faculties. As humankind asks for and allows my angelic assistance, you will become more *as* the Angels in truth, and less dependent on our assistance. So there will come a time when you express the attributes of the Angels by choice and through your own desire and personal growth.

We of the Angelic Realm know this day will come and are joyous beyond words at this prospect, for indeed this will be Heaven on Earth, our glorious Freedom Star. Ever has it been our task to assist you in becoming and expressing your full potential. These our gifts to you are indeed transformative gifts. Your request for and use of these gifts have far reaching effects on your being, your bodies. These gifts open you to your spark of God within, create great advances in awareness, and transform you on all levels, from within to without.

Call me, Lolijael, for the vision to continue, to know you are going in the right direction. Life can be a harsh taskmaster, often far harder than you could ever have known. Nothing is given you that you cannot manage, though often you refuse to believe this. Ask and I will infuse you with the will and energy to continue and complete, or to see a way to transform the activity into a pleasurable and supportive one. I am Lolijael, your Angel of Persistence, at your service. ✿

Lolijael
Angel of Persistance

Segment Five

13 Angels

Angel of Sound, Bellarias
Angel of Intent, Delicielle
Angel of Hope, Volachek
Angel of Inner Child, Melijael
Angel of Going Home, Hoirael
Angel of Health, Anuziel
Angel of Bliss, Havilon
Angel of Music, Liriel
Angel of Harmony, Amberelle
Angel of Freedom, Hilo
Angel of Awareness, Sartagene
Angel of Team Love, Anrisael
Angel of Balance, Sihilon

Bellarias

Angel of Sound

$\boxed{\text{A}}$ccept my glow now as I meld and melt into your throat chakra, for I am the Angel of Sound, Bellarias (*bel lar' ee as'*). Feel the tones and frequencies that I bring you as God's gift to humanity now in this time of growth to Oneness.

I, Bellarias, come as a messenger bearing gifts to realign, balance, and heal your physical, emotional, and mental bodies. *Ask and I will gladly assist you with a cosmic tune up.* I come with healing frequencies, sounds that gently and powerfully reset your internal systems, via sound, returning the mechanisms and the programs that operate these systems to perfect function. Emotionally you will feel soothed and peaceful, mentally clear and alert.

These healing frequencies are as a refreshing, regenerative bath. On your request, my healing energies meld with your energies, gently realigning your internal workings. You may notice little change initially, for you generally lose memory quickly of discomforts no longer present. On checking yourself, very likely you *will* notice that you do indeed feel clear, stable and energetic.

Much can be achieved with these sound frequencies as you continue to accept this gift and open to the changes within. Latent abilities will gradually begin to operate and your life *can* evolve into a magical existence. Call me, my friend. I am Bellarias, at your service - your Angel of Sound. ✿

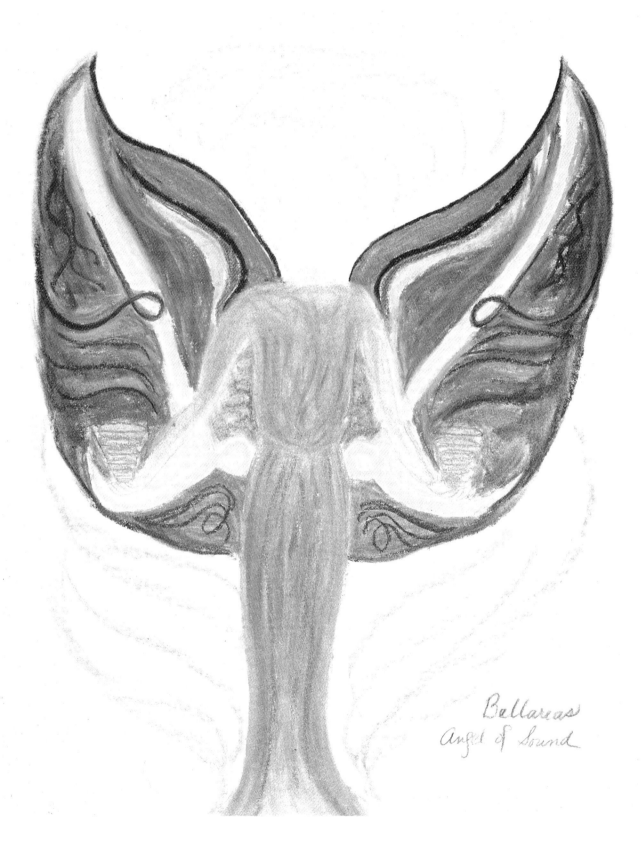

Bellareas
angel of Sound

Delicielle

Angel of Intent

onscious intending is a powerful tool to create the life you want. I am Delicielle, your Angel of Intent, here to help you understand and apply this conceptual tool. Intend clearly to accomplish most easily what you desire. Understand that with the current rise of earthly frequencies, intentions powerfully and quickly create your realities.

My energies are delicate and gentle, soft and feminine. My essence is like pure crystal tones. I am the Angel of Intent, of delicate beginnings, of new germinations. My ministrations are from the hub of creation, gently gathering the emerging threads of energy, nurturing their growth, until they can be handed over to the appropriate being to further develop and mature these creations. Softly and gently, I tend these threads of energy, gently separating them, nurturing their growth, noting their energy values, as I call in the appropriate receiver for these threads of creation. I am Delicielle (*deh lee' see el'*), your Angel of gentle, delicate beginnings, gently encouraging and nurturing new thought patterns, new feelings, new creations.

I am Delicielle, gentle of touch, soft of nature, present now to gently assist you in your growth. I do *not* initiate change, but gently nurture new growth to strength, gently guiding the first moments of change, guiding new insights and implementations. My work is like microsurgery at the cusp of creation.

Delicielle
Angel of Intent

When a new idea begins to grow inside of you, call on me to gently coax it forward, to bring it to light and clarity. As you go about your various activities, open to the new ways of doing these activities, to new insights. At your request, I will gently help these insights come boldly forward in your awareness. These new insights are frequently delicate and easily crushed, and swept away. My energies can bring these insights and budding creations to strength in your awareness.

My energies are also intended to nurture unassigned budding creational energies. As I tend these growing energies, I call forth you who wish these energies and match these budding creations to your recipient energies. I nurture these diverse energies as they grow in strength and differentiate into distinct values, until I gently hand them over to appropriate recipients, releasing them wholly to your Being. I am Delicielle, present to meld these budding energies to your desires, your creational choices. Invite my energies and my sharing into your life, and I will share generously of these creative energies. Invite my energies to strengthen your creative abilities, your insight, your intuitive flexing. I gladly share my energies with all who ask.

Your part in this cocreation is to allow my nurturing energies and assist, side by side, then continue to guide your creation to completeness. I offer gentle nudges along the way to assure your finish. Ask and I shall help. Call and I will be there, ever eager to assist in the birth of new ideas, new growth patterns, and gentle changes. I am Delicielle, your Angel of Intent. ✿

Intend clearly to accomplish most easily what you desire.

~Angel Delicielle.

Volachek

Angel of Hope

H ope is the hand for which one in despair pleads and gropes, dimly tries to envision. One with no hope does indeed feel lost and abandoned, lethargic unto death. To believe again that life can be hopeful, that a new direction is within reach and within the strength and ability of the searcher, is the first step to change, the first step on the way home.

Allow my nurturing, generative energies to enfold and permeate your heart as I uplift your soul and soften your mind to show the way. I am Volachek (*vo la chek'*), your Angel of Hope, at your service to open your eyes to new possibilities, to put a shoulder to your load, and build your hope for life. Call me, when you see no alternatives and feel there is no way out. Call me when you can't move forward and want to quit on life. Open to feel hope like the first buds in very early spring open in hopeful expectancy of sunlight seeping through the cold morning air. Feel my crystalline light bringing a hopeful sparkle to your awareness. I begin movement from inertia, with my shoulder to the potential crack in awareness.

Let me help you smile again, open your awareness to more supportive choices, boost your will to live and love again. My energies will help you get on track again, and live life joyfully, sharing hope and bliss with others. I joyfully offer you my service of hope to assist you in growth and service to others. Seeing the Light of Hope ignite in another's eyes is a great joy to all. Call me. Open to my joyful help, for yourself or others. I am Volachek. ✩

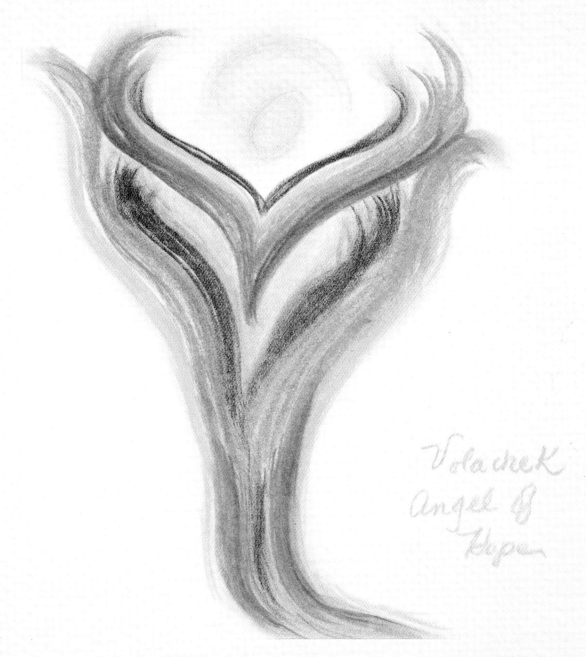

Volachek
angel of
Hope

E A Terry
© 10/93

Melijael

Angel of Inner Child

I, Melijael (*Mee li' jay el'*), the Angel of your Inner Child, descends to Earth, playful and childlike, holding the essence of the Inner Child in all of you. My energy lovingly nurtures your inner child. This inner child aspect of each of you often emotionally rules and directs your lives. Know all of your efforts in life are productive, every step appreciated. Taking steps, making the effort, is the essential element. Each step helps you hone your creation, uncovers another layer of the puzzle, opens another doorway of Light. Perfection is achieved on this plane in degrees. Goals always have subsequent goals.

Look inside. Acknowledge your inner child. I offer my loving ministrations to assist you with your own self acceptance for the innocence and love this child holds. Be kind and gentle with yourself as you gently soothe the hurts away. Gently and lovingly walk, talk, listen, laugh, play, and feel again. This child is part of you that you left behind, in pain, scarred by life, abandoned and rejected, when only good intentions were meant. Accept again this innocent child that you separated and rejected, when you decided to grow up. Open yourself to my loving assistance and I will help open your heart to this acceptance and appreciation of your inner self, the child within.

Take time and care to love and appreciate your inner child, with all its attributes, even as I do. Gently bring this part of yourself to peace and joy. Allow me to gently

Melijael
Angel of Inner Child

and lovingly satisfy your childish longings for soothing, reassuring hugs. Allow this, your inner child, to bask in my loving acceptance. Create the time and space to satisfy these needs, for indeed they are yours as well.

This self acceptance allows a miraculous unfolding and refocusing of all your life energies. This moment of lovingly directed self appreciation, unconditionally given and joyous accepted, is a pivotal point in life all long for. Bringing your inner child to peace and joy permits you to begin to look outside of yourselves. I am your Angel of the Inner Child and I offer nurturing energies to *all* of humanity. Become playful again. Laugh. Dance. Feel the joy of my total loving appreciation of who you are and all you do. I am your partner in this. Dance with me.

Together we can heal and uplift this child to loving acceptance of the greater you. This reciprocal acceptance of all parts of yourself opens magical doorways. I, Melijael, await your call. ✿

Hoirael

Angel of Going Home

ear one, do you hear the call? Your Father is calling you Home. You are missed and needed at Home. Yes, *you* are needed at home to complete the circle. God's heart is full to overflowing with Love for you who sunk the deepest into the densities here on Earth. Be at ease, my friend, for all of life is a striving, steps toward home. It's not who wins, but how the game is played. God is always appreciative of every step you take, always loving you for the purity of your essence, and celebrating each corner you round in life. You gave the most. You took the hardest jobs, played the most thankless roles, and are asked to awaken now and shine your light even within the deepest densities of Earth. Wake up! Hear this call. Remember!

As you descended into the darkest crannies of the Earth, and took on the heaviest karma, we all knew you would forget. Some of you may not recognize your call to go home, so long have you maintained your roles in the depth of the darkness. Remember. You coded yourself to remember at this time, to go home at this time. The war is over, the play is ended, the game is done. Now you can go home, having played a great role.

All of God's children are called to return home now. *All!* If you hear this at all, if this crosses your path, if someone mentions this to you, *you* are being called. Not someone that you may consider more spiritual, a nicer person, but *you!* Hear the call. Relax and open to the pull to return home. You have done well. Breathe deeply of the appreciation from all of creation, and *consider retiring to heaven.*

I am Hoirael (*hoy ra' el'*), your Angel of Going Home and your honorary escort, to ease your journey, to comfort your soul, to shower you with the appreciation of the legions of Angels. *Well done!!* Now you can rest and celebrate. Time to go home. Your Father awaits you. Welcomes you. Yours is a hero's welcome. All of creation heralds your homecoming and blesses you for a job well done. You have earned your place in heaven. Go home, my friend, with honors. We salute you and thank you. God blesses you. No celebration will surpass the one that awaits you with the Father. Return to the arms and comfort, to the love of the Father.

I, Hoirael, await your call. It is my honor to assist you in returning home. I am at your service, your Angel of Going Home. ✿

Doirael
Angel of
Going Home

Anuziel

Angel of Health

I, Anuziel (*a noo' zee el'*), the Angel of Health, request permission to share my gifts. A lack of perfect energy flow in the physical, emotional, and mental human bodies will create less than perfection in these bodies. *Health* refers to healed, complete in perfection, and flowing in loving energies of life. Perfect health supports and makes possible the experiences of pleasure, joy, love, bliss, strength, and clarity.

I, the Angel of (perfect) Health, am here to assist in the perfection of the energy flows always present in perfect health. Know that perfect health comes as a result of the healed mental and emotional bodies, as you progress on the journey home. With perfection of health, your sole purpose in life becomes the journey home, the path of Oneness, and assisting others on this same path.

I, Anuziel, step forward early on this path to assist, if the call but comes for my help. Ever present and attentive, I am the great facilitator, consoler, and physician. I am the great clarifier, for illness, lack of perfection, is humanity's own creation. Call me as your need becomes apparent. Call on me for energy, for clarity, to know the 'how' and 'why' of your condition, and to recreate the reality of health within and without. Embrace the flow of love and joy that I enliven in your heart. Create and urge the flow and expansion of this love. Allow the loving embrace of this love, for indeed *Love* is the great healer. The great flow of the Love of God, the knowledge of unity with God and all of creation, brings the wisdom of the ages to your doorstep, to your awareness.

Acknowledgment of your own creation and, therefore, your own responsibility to change from within to affect outer change is your part, your role. I offer my assistance to create perfection in the moment, for once you remember how to create health, the choice is then yours. You can create health to the extent you choose.

Anuziel
Angel of Health

Call on me and allow my loving ministrations to embrace you and your world, to help you create the perfection you desire. Recreate with me the loving, glowing person that is more truthfully who you are. Be perfection, feel perfection, know perfection. Allow the softening of the heart and the welling up of Love and all feelings from within.

Create and allow, even encourage the flow of love and joy, but acknowledge other emotions as well, feeling them, even embracing them, blessing them for the opportunity they created. Then let them go, releasing all feelings and conditions. Release the old patterns. Choose now perfection of mind, heart, body, and soul, for indeed, you do choose your reality and you do create it. Choose consciously from love to hold the perfection in all bodies as you flow back to the Heart of God.

Feel this peace and stillness that descends upon you as I work with you. Feel the aligning of the chakras, the energy centers and the gentle shifts to balance. Feel the peace of the ages with the perfect balance of your bodies in perfect harmony. As I, Anuziel, embody your bodies, I bring peace, while balancing, aligning, opening, shifting all energies into the balance needed for perfect energy flow and balanced awareness. Quiet time is requested with some rest period best afterwards. I am ever grateful for the opportunity to work my magic with humanity. Call me to assist in time of need or in desire for greater perfection. You are my joy. I am your loving, healing assistant, Anuziel.

I reflect the energies of spring when creation is resplendent in growth and bloom. My energies create change to original intent and pattern. My essence, while feminine, will meet the need of the caller and receiver of my energies, for indeed I will embody those energies most needed by the caller, be it masculine or feminine.

The memory of my experience with you becomes a part of you, to be called upon at will and, therefore, help you be more responsible and active in maintaining and furthering your own health. Indeed, the memory will be cellular and further imprinted in each of your bodies, physical, emotional, mental, and spiritual. With coparticipation and increasing awareness, the realization and appreciation of these changes will continue and improve. A lack of this awareness may cause fading of these results. Further quiet time with the request for further assistance will surely bring my continued ministrations and joyous exchange.

I am ever at your service and eager to assist. Do call on me and know you have the innate power to change your world and reality, and to maintain this perfection in the joy of life and love with the Father. I await your call. ✿

Havilon

Angel of Bliss

Bliss is unabridged joy and happiness, well anchored in the physical body and radiating through the emotional, mental, and spiritual bodies. Bliss may occur with the rise of kundalini and be felt like an explosion, moving outward from the heart and lower emotional centers, breaking patterns of fear and creating bliss. Or you may open and balance all of your energy centers, and breathe and move your energies. Then flowing the life force unimpeded through your physical body, radiate this energy through the emotional, mental and spiritual bodies, creating a pervasive soft glow of bliss that thrills the universe even as you feel wonderfully elated and happy.

Living and moving in bliss have far reaching effects within yourself and the world as you know it, creating radiant changes in relationships, society and among all the kingdoms of Earth. This experience of bliss will release all need for control in your world, for none will feel another has what they desire, but can not have. Love abounds when all act from this field of bliss.

I am Havilon (*ha va lon'*), your Angel of Bliss. Open your minds to my gift, all you who suffer boredom and mediocrity, all who desire change, all of you grasping for a piece of joy in your world of pain. Call me to assist as you open your minds and hearts to the greater transcendent qualities of bliss, at which recreational drugs and activities only hint. You *are* all you need for this experience of bliss.

Request my assistance to move in the flow of bliss, in gratitude for the blessings of this gift accepting it as your birth right, your heritage. Accept this as being an appropriate and desired state to create life in perfection. Bliss supports and is part of the basis of perfect health, relationships that serve others as their reason for existence, and love of all creation.

Allow me to encourage this blissful experience in your life. Call me, Havilon, and feel the bubbling energy of bliss awaken within you. I await your call in blissful anticipation. ✿

Havilon
Angel of Bliss

Liriel

Angel of Music

I, Liriel (*li ree el'*), the Angel of Music, offer my services to open your pathways of hearing the celestial realms of universal music. This music is enchanting and transformative, in that it resets patterns to original intention and uplifts the soul to new heights of awareness. With my help, humans can once again converse with all the kingdoms of Earth, animals, plants and minerals alike.

My gentle ministrations open your 'ears' to the music of the spheres, to higher frequencies. Music can sway the soul, open and bathe your inner being with gentle, healing soothing tones. The tones and timber of an individual's voice can be healing sounds to another. Allow my assistance to gently culture your voice, open your awareness to its effect on yourself and your surroundings, and bring it to optimum efficiency. You are blessed with an incredible instrument of sound, each of you. Know your voice can heal another, can uplift another's heart and soul, and open new doorways of awareness as you direct your energies lovingly through your voice.

A kind word, a soothing phrase, an uplifting inquiry can set the pace for another's entire life. The effects of your spoken word, your intentions manifesting through the music of your voice, ripple out from you as a stone tossed in a pond. Use your God given musical instrument, your voice, to create and share the music of the Angels as you share and uplift, help another with a kind word, with praise for the beauty that they are, for taking part in this play of life with you.

Liriel
Angel of Music

My assistance melded with your intentions will create miracles in your life and all around you. Invite my help. I am able to create and direct an entire range of sounds and effects that are grand in scope. My crescendos and diminuendos dance across all times. Just call my name and I will help temper your voice, soften your response, gentle your reply, or strengthen your intent, whatever is needed in the moment. I am Liriel, your Angel of Music, ready to create your own personal music with you. I am at your service, musically so. I am Liriel. ✿

You are blessed with an incredible instrument of sound,
  each of you . . .

                                                        ~Angel Liriel.

Amberelle

Angel of Harmony

armony is a golden, blessed, peaceful and joyous exchange of energies, thick with harmonic energies anchoring within you. Even as you laugh and open your arms to this golden energy, I, Amberelle (*am' ber el'*), will bless you with this sparkle and energetic essence to laugh and embrace the purity and blessedness of this very moment. Feel the warmth, the glow of love that flows through you as I join you, a chosen comrade on this journey home. Ever will I, Amberelle, be present to assist and bring harmony and joy to all relations and all changes.

I can be with you always and throughout your Being, for I am your true nature. I am nurturing and supportive of your true essence, as I smooth your life path. Call on me always, and especially when joy seems foreign or an experience of the past. Forever will I joyfully support and build the harmonious layers within and without, that all of life may be a joy to live and a gift to God. Harmony brings joy and clarity of purpose, ease of living, and blessedness to the soul.

Feel the Light that you are, the buoyancy, the feeling of lightness. I am warm and joyful like an opening bloom, the rising of the essence of the flower, the full ascension of the energies, a deep gold with light sparkling through it, golden Angel dust showering your joyful face. Feel the radiance of golden energy that permeates you as you call me, Amberelle, your Angel of Harmony. I await your call in glowing anticipation. ✿

Amberelle
Angel of Harmony

Hilo

Angel of Freedom

ong have I, Hilo (*hi' lo'*), waited for the opportunity to assist humans in your quest for *freedom*. Long and hard have you fought for freedom, straining to unshackle your souls. Few of you have come to a sense of real freedom in your lives, for often one slavedom has been traded for another, as you continually assign others your rights and responsibilities, giving away your rights to all of the experts that you believe know more than you and can make life right.

These 'experts' barter your rights with your silent approval. You have become a slave to your monetary and other belief systems, believing you need to accumulate more and more money. This you innocently believe will bring you joy. These choices with no joy are sucking your life force, as slowly and inevitably your enthusiasm in life deflates. Almost as if awakening from a dream, you look around to find how to invest your energies and create the freedom that supports life at its fullest.

I am your Angel of Freedom, here to assist you in rediscovering your sense of freedom, your inner and outer freedom. Call me, your Angel of Freedom, to help you see how you *can* change inside, you can *begin to be your joy* and still meet your chosen responsibilities. *Take the time to feel and heal, for therein lies your freedom.* No thing or activity outside of yourself creates freedom. Open to the inner healing that releases you to a peaceful freedom within. Make the inner changes that will create the freedom to be fully who you are now.

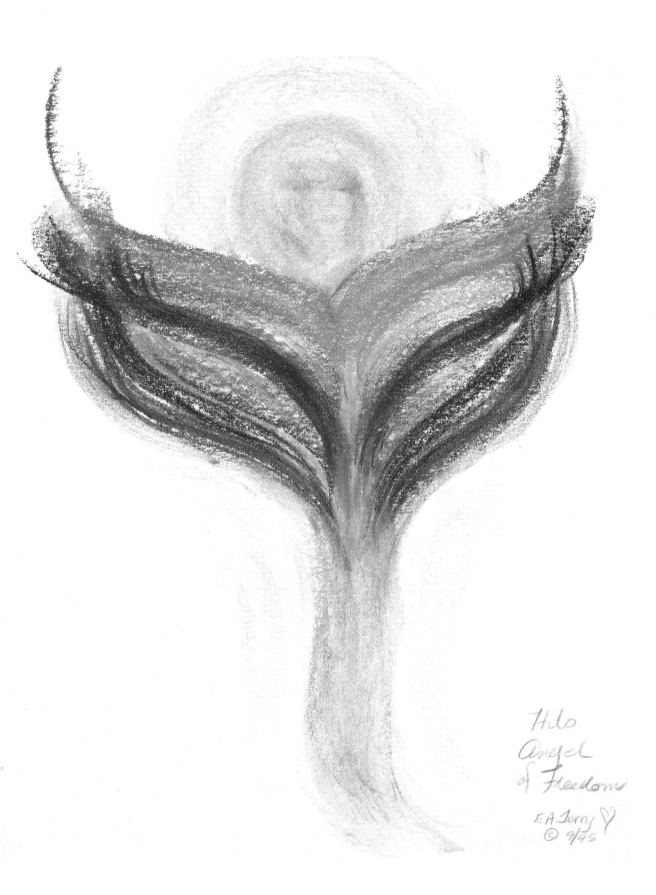

Hilo
Angel
of Freedom

E A Terry ♥
© 9/95

Take my hand and move into your joy. Feel my gentle nudge, feel the urge to choose differently as you live your everyday life. Taste the joy and enthusiasm of living that are aligned to your energies and the gifts *you* bring to Earth now. Feel who you are fully and embrace *you* inside, allowing all that you are to surface for recognition and appreciation. Open to the joy of union with all of creation, freedom in Oneness. Try this. Devote several hours a week to an activity that brings you joy.

I can feel that some of you feel you are at the bottom of the barrel, the end of your rope. You have worked hard to achieve, you have sacrificed much of your life, tried to follow commonly believed guidance, and all for naught. You feel empty, abandoned, joyless. You really do not know what will bring you joy, because you've used the last option you knew.

Dear one, please allow my added energies, my insight to uplift your soul, to open your mind to new alternatives and quicken your heart to know that joy *can* be yours again, now! Call on me, your Angel of Freedom. My assistance is yours for the asking. Long have I awaited your call. Your soul has been patient as your ego quested for joy. Now, blessed one, allow my assistance and try my guidance. Take one step at a time and feel the joy begin to once again unfold within your heart.

Open to the guidance from God that has been put in your path. Open your mind and heart to feel what could be joyful, pleasant. Allow and encourage the inner healing, to feel joy again, to know 'pleasant' again. Once your healing begins, you may be able to move outside of your self and choose to share a talent with others. Invite my assistance to nudge this process forward. Let it grow and flower in your mind. Breathe in this new reality, this joy in your life, for you will discover that assisting others can be a real joy.

As new ideas slip into your mind, jot them down. You may find some are interrelated and support one main idea, and ways to move in your new direction. Some may seem unrelated, but may apply to later activities that you choose. Freedom, dear soul, is a state of mind, and this freedom flourishes in joy. Past choices have created your present life. Choose to move in truth and joy to create a life of freedom.

I am Hilo, your Angel of Freedom. I await your call. ✿

Sartagene

Angel of Awareness

A ll human life on Earth is a striving for awareness. Upon descent into your human body, much of your awareness was erased, veiled by your own hand, to create the innocence needed to grow through the experiences you yourself planned and now direct from on high. Slowly, through the layers, your awareness is emerging again to the illusoriness of this existence and your unity with God. A grand play, all planned to impel you through growth in this density, and to know God within *while in this density,* to turn back inward from the world without to the reality within.

I, Sartagene (*sar ta' ge nee'*), your Angel of Awareness, gladly sprinkle my energies through your life to open your mind and heart to ever greater realities, beliefs, and values. Always choice remains to embrace or reject new awarenesses. Truth will pull you forward. Your physical body knows truth and speaks clearly back to you its evaluation, truth bringing openness and joy, untruth bringing stagnation and confusion. Allow the flow, the movement and recognition of this emotional and physical response to truth and opening awareness. This *is* life. This opening awareness is growth through life, on your journey home to God. God, who is only you, within. A short trip, if you but open your awareness to *this* truth.

Your times are accelerating. Your awareness has been quickened to embrace your emerging truths more readily, to allow *'AHA!'* experiences more often, to welcome quickly now the probability of rapidly changing realities. No paradigm of living is now 'safe' from changing realities.

Open your heart and mind, dear soul, to your own greatest gift to you, to your own awakening to who you really are, and why you are here on Earth. My energies will boost this growing awareness of yours, the emerging questing, the curiosity that is peeking out now to know your place in this creation.

Allow me to help you emerge from your mental inertia, or from your clamoring mental activity into knowingness. Ask and I will assist you, help you connect to your own intuition (and yes, *everyone* has the faculty, all be it, mightily denied by many). Just feel your being as you consider a 'fact,' and with understanding and openness in your mind, you will feel and know if this is also your truth.

Awareness is openness, inward and outward simultaneously. The result, with practice and possibly some 'house cleaning,' is knowingness. Question and then be still and know your answer. Be receptive. My assistance will urge your knowingness to become known to you. Awareness will allow you to relax rigidities of thought and the physical body, of emotional patterns no longer useful, of beliefs no longer truthful for you.

I am your Angel of Awareness here with your wake up call. Awaken and stretch into your new awareness. Welcome Home! We hope you enjoyed the Earthly journey. Well acted, we would say. Some fellow actors may yet need your or my waking touch to move into the reality of God within. Be gentle within and without, as your awareness expands. Be gentle with others who are more sleepy. One word or touch in love or support opens entire new worlds, as you reach out and share with another your new found awareness.

Breathe and move, dance through life now, in full knowing, with clear purpose, with the energy and means to move mountains, to uplift fellow souls in joy. Open your own mind to the gifts of others, to their unique and exquisite dance through life. Enjoy this dance together, for the grand culmination of this creative phase is near. And you starred in it! Good show!

Open to my energies of dawning awareness, of shifting insights, and innate knowingness, all you who suffer stagnation in mind and soul, heart and body. Remember to call me, Sartagene, when you feel the itch for movement and change. I await your invitation. I am Sartagene, your Angel of Awareness, ready to assist. ✿

Sartagene
Angel of
Awareness

Anrisael

Angel of Team Love

D ear one, I address you directly to re-enliven your desire and abilities to flow, swim, and fly in the joy of creative love with another of equal standing and desires. Long have you and many others yearned for the joy of openly exchanging, giving and receiving loving energies, of knowing and feeling the full flow of loving energies, understanding another fully, dancing in the joy of singularity and togetherness at once.

The full acceptance of one's self, indeed, self love, with appreciation and understanding of all aspects of one's self, opens and qualifies one for *flowing* (used as a verb as in moving) loving energies with another, even many others.

I speak to all of humanity when I say this aspect of love, *team love*, begs attention to heal and be whole again. Open your heart and mind to the possibilities of this in your life. Your questioning is noted, and as you grow in the ability to be in this team relationship with comfort and joy, with self acceptance and self worth, with appreciation of and loving interaction with your partner.

Your life now will accurately guide you to open old wounds and heal them. Continue your paced healing, your gentle unfolding of your history, going back to feelings that imprinted in tense moments. Compassionately allow yourself to heal as you bless yourself and all others, to know all was for growth. Find your lessons.

Anriuael,
Angel of
Team Love

Understand your accomplices and thank them, one and all, for playing their parts so well in your life dramas, and release them. Then turn your loving attention on yourself, blessing yourself and appreciating yourself, for the jobs and parts in the plays were well done. No rights or wrongs, only lessons.

Then the lessons change. No longer are the same lessons needed as they were previously. A team partner becomes the next player to play the next play: *team love*, partnering at its best. Trust and understanding at its best. Cooperation at its best. Love and appreciation at its height, all balanced and flexible.

As a partner in this level of team relationship, you are fully centered and balanced emotionally, physically, mentally and spiritually. Clear and bright, you and your peers are also in full partnership with your Higher Selves and God. Intimacy is in full blossom within your relationship. The synergy of your relationship is joyfully powerful and in sync, so that all of creation seems to flow with your team. You move and create with the grace and speed of the Angels. Thus my gift as the Angel of Team Love, that I support and engender this level of team relationship, this level of fun and joy in life.

Allow your past with all of its hurts and anguish, its sorrow and sadness, its anger and rage to come up and bless it and release it. Thank God and all of your previous partners for their assistance in your lessons. Allow your heart and mind to open to the possibilities now of moving toward a balanced relationship of team love with appreciation, cooperation and support, joy and bliss.

Feel the joy of this possibility, the graceful flow of cooperation, the easy understanding and appreciation of your partner and they for you, the outward stroke of activities as you weave your energies together in spontaneous creation. Feel the clearly stated, fully heard, and openly accepted communications between partners. Feel these possibilities and move into them now. I joyfully offer my assistance to expand you into these possibilities. I am Anrisael (*an ree' say el'*), your Angel of Team Love, ready and eager to assist you in your team relationships. I await your call. ✧

Sihilon

Angel of Balance

I, Sihilon (*see hee' lon'*) come to you now from the Angelic Realms to share my gift of perfect balance. My energies of balance assist in bringing the physical, mental, emotional and spiritual bodies into perfect balance and alignment. Allow my help in taking your life force energies to higher levels of balance within the chakras, the energy centers of the body. These will become balanced within and integrated with each other, for smooth efficient functioning of your human body, far beyond what is common on Earth now.

I assist in balancing all chakras, and especially the second chakra, to balance the energy of the male and female in all humans. This balance of the male and female energies that is reached within *each* individual, regardless of gender, is essential to balanced living now, for this relaxes much of the 'tug a war' energy that exists in relationships. I work with the integrative energy systems of the body, with the balancing energy of the gold life force ray, and with the heart and soul of the individual to bring resolution in all areas for perfect balance.

The balanced flow of these energies from and between all bodies and even from Earth and God gives perfect fluidity and surety to all movement. This will give you blessed souls in human bodies a taste of our angelic clarity of thoughts and intentions, our expanded capacity through the heart chakra, and our fluidity of movement in total poise and agility from dimension to dimension and from location to time. No boundaries. This will open the doors to relationships in pure joy and perfect balance, energized with divine guidance and blessed results.

I bring you the angelic freedom of movement in all ways. Complete control of all movement, through all bodies of energy with fluidity and flexibility, far surpassing previous possibilities. Feel my energies as I share fluid flexibility, surety of expressions, musical movements of the physical body as you spiral into your true balance. The balanced physical body is the result of the balanced and integrated wholeness of the physical, mental, emotional and spiritual bodies. This will feel new to many of you, as a first time experience, but know this is to become the norm as you come into your own perfect balance.

Feel life as a dance of magic. Pirouette into your bliss with the fullness of your balanced life energies. This added angelic facilitation heightens the athlete's prowess beyond all known limits. Call me for assistance with movement in bliss and joy.

Feel the joy of your bodies, as they begin to move *in sync* with all of creation. All of you with aches and pains, stiff joints, anguish and sorrow, lackluster and joylessness, call my energies to begin movement, to assist with a step at a time. Allow my ministering energies to open your eyes, hearts, and bodies to incredible opportunities of joy in movement, bliss in flight with the more integrated, balanced functioning within your bodies and with all of creation.

I am Sihilon, your Angel of perfect Balance, at your service to tweak your bodies into perfect alignment and balance, and to spur your energies to flight. Allow my loving fluid ministrations to heal your stiffness, your aches, your inertia, your lethargy. My greatest joy is your flight of bliss. Only ask, and I am at your service. I am here, ever present, ever watchful for the caller of my energies. Call me for your own bodies or direct me to another in need. I am hopeful that my energies will cause an avalanche of health and an explosion of creation as the energies of Oneness flood your being.

A great movement is afoot. Join the crowd and take flight in all aspects of your being. Call me with joy and expectancy and I will boost your energies with mine. I am Sihilon, at your service in joyful bliss. ✿

Sihilon
Angel of
Balance

Segment Six

13 Angels

Angel of Prosperity, Lenarius
Angel of Clarity, Conae
Angel of Compassion, Roselle
Angel of Direction, Pralunizak
Angel of Tolerance, Anrisnoel
Angel of Growth, Esofael
Angel of Light, Anrisielle
Angel of Universal Love, Larmeo
Angel of Acceleration, Hillilael
Angel of Trust, Naomaelle
Angel of Sleep, Anjeeliel
Angel of Beauty, Elicenoel
Angel of Transition, Menowrael

Lenarius

Angel of Prosperity

W hen a need of more prosperity is perceived, you *are* activating the call to me, Lenarius *(le na' ree us')*, Angel of Prosperity, if you but look toward The Creator in these times of need.

Prosperity might be defined as having whatever is needed whenever it is needed, the fullness and knowingness that you are provided for in every moment, *and* that you are a cocreator of your reality with free will. This free will includes the choice of accepting the prosperity of God so freely offered in Love.

Call me now, your Angel of Prosperity, to fuse your relationship with God, the knowing of the fullness of God's Love, the joy of the unrestricted flow of His Love in your life. Prosperity requires flow of the Love energy, a giving and receiving, without end. No shortage. You are given all that you ask, if you but allow the receiving and become part of the giving as well.

Indeed, the giver is blessed in equal measure as the receiver, as the giver's heart expands and energetically connects with the receiver and God. You are the precious children of God and it is His joy and pleasure to gift you in all, to cocreate with you in the joy and flow of fullness. The secret of prosperity is the creational cycling of the energies, the give and take, with the knowingness of plenty.

Lenaria
Angel of
Prosperity

A.E.Jerry ♡ © 10/95

Join the team. Be a conscious cocreator with God. I, Lenarius, your Angel of Prosperity, will energize and support this exchange with all the angelic energies at my disposal. Many of you have become self-serving and hurtful of your brothers in your zeal to amass transient things here on Earth. Know that true prosperity is just the flow of the energy of knowing all things and energies are yours, if you but join the Heart of God. Service in Love allows fullness of joy and prosperity when your beliefs permit this flow.

I am your Angel of Prosperity. Call me now and I will infuse your being with the knowingness of the unlimited wealth within. Your heart will know no bounds as you embrace your truth, your divine reality. I embrace your heart in love and joy, in fullness of prosperity and unlimited wealth. My energies are powerful and yet gentle. I am at your service. I am Lenarius. ✿

Conae

Angel of Clarity

I am Conae *(co nay'),* your Angel of Clarity, and I wish to offer my assistance now to help clear the static fog from your perceptions. Indeed, incoming communication bombards your senses at all times, whether in conscious waking state or sleep. Those of you becoming more aware, awakening inside, may feel inept at receiving these higher frequencies being shared with you. Humanity has hidden behind its veils for eons, and as these barriers recede, awareness and knowingness begin to return, bit by bit.

I come to you now to speed the resolution of your reception, clear the picture, heighten the colors, and sharpen your overall ability to receive. These mechanisms of reception have been 'off-line' for a very long time. My energies are as an engineer reawakening a machine long in disuse, tweaking this valve, turning this knob, reconnecting this energy conduit, resetting programs. A useful assistant at this time, would you agree?

Call me to assist you now, for indeed, your awareness is already opening substantially, as you have come to these words, and are using this book. A little overhaul with my loving energies will go a long way in helping your energies to flow smoothly and your entire persona to benefit from your personal growth in an easy, comfortable, and efficient way.

As your Angel of Clarity, I am here to strengthen your body systems to receive this incoming knowledge more clearly. Often, as your innate knowingness grows, as your intuition blossoms, your outward attention may push this away as a bother. You may feel the intuitive tug as an irritation, and continue to push this 'under the rug,' ignoring this quiet insistent voice of truth, which you later realize has been with you for a very long time.

I bring clarity to this voice. I bring personal awareness that this voice is your personal guidance system, and not merely an abnormality within yourself that is bothersome. Open to my ministrations and join the ranks of clear, receptive Light workers already active on Earth. Invite my assistance and I will gladly join you to open and clear your receptive channels to your optimum operating ability, always tempered to your personal growth and abilities.

Some of you are just now beginning to open within, to know that your body is insistently talking to you, to feel stronger in your views, and open to appreciation of others' feelings. I feel your ache for the connections within, the open communication channels of knowingness, of feeling in *sync* with others, of easy flow in your activities and exchanges. I openly offer my energies of clarity to assist you gently in seeing, knowing, hearing, and *being* more fully and clearly.

If you are eager for this faculty to blossom within, I offer you my loving ministrations. Call me to set up the communion and clarity of the Angels within you. Together we can soar as you test and strengthen your abilities. Your clarity and independence are your gift to me, your Angel of Clarity. My channels are open. I am at your service, Conae, your Angel of Clarity. ✿

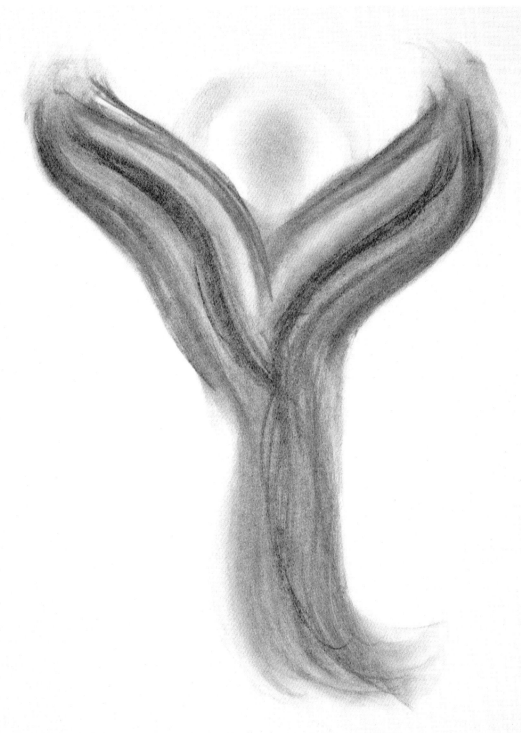

Conae
Angel of Clarity

Roselle

Angel of Compassion

any of you would benefit from the compassionate embrace of my Light and Love. Let me uplift your tender heart and soothe your troubled mind with my loving embrace. I know your turmoil and sorrow as my own and entreat you to feel and know now my caring, compassionate, and loving embrace. Allow me to sweep you into the loving space where I can comfort your troubled soul.

I am Roselle (*rose el'*), your Angel of Compassion. Allow my help to feel your pain and emerge from it, changed and healed. I am at your service. When I add my essence to yours, you are strong enough to feel your pain, go through it, and release it in joy and love. My compassion is your transformative opportunity..

Come to me, your Angel of Compassion, those of you in the throes of sorrow, pain, loss, and anguish. Allow my compassionate embrace and I will bring soothing comfort to your embittered soul. I know your hopelessness as my own. I feel your joyless life as my burden. I live beside you as you strive to be happy and joyful in loss and pain. I love you with the tenderness of a mother and the strength of a father. Allow my embrace, my soothing energies to ease your burdens and lighten your heart, to open your mind to know the inner Light and Love of God. I am with you always.

Call on me now. Just ask and I am ever with you, embracing you, putting a shoulder to your load, infusing you with the energy to smile and expand in love. Go

216

Roselle
Angel of
Compassion

forward now with my strength of resolve and compassion. Know you have this loving friend at your side and in your heart to help, to allow the feelings, to bear the burdens and emerge transformed, stronger, brighter, more clear.

I am Roselle and ever at your service, if you but call--my line is always open to you. As you allow my help, my energies to blend with yours, my compassion blossoms in love for yourself and others, for compassion is an aspect of love on Earth. Compassion opens the door to be of service to others, to assist others to rise out of their struggle in life, into the ease of living in love. Reach out to another, once you have felt my help, for I am ever with you, continuing to assist you and ever eager to help others. You will find this an even greater gift than my initial assistance to you. I welcome you to my team! I am Roselle, your Angel of Compassion. ✿

Pralunizak

Angel of Direction

Often times you feel sad and despondent, disconnected from reality, as a ship without sail or rudder. The mists and haze in your awareness are like a fog that clouds direction, so that you doubt even which way to go. Just formulating a next step becomes an impossibility and more than you can bear.

In times of doubt and despair, I offer my services of clear direction, for I am Pralunizak (*prah loo' ni zak'*), your Angel of Direction. Clearly I see outcomes and available possibilities, often clouded from your viewpoint, from which you may choose. I offer to clarify your awareness, boost your openness, encourage your resolve, and nudge you forward into a possibility that can definitively lift your veils and open your knowingness, your surety of your right direction.

Great are the energies available to you as you partake of these angelic gifts. My gift is to help you direct these new energies into uplifting and evolutionary directions that best suit your chosen growth cycles. While these energy gifts are precious and wonderful, they are powerful in affecting life, and supporting changes when given proper direction.

Dear soul, allow my assistance, that you may garner the greatest value from these my angelic gifts. I ask that you choose consciously, and open to my gentle guidance as you feel and grow accustomed to these new energies growing inside of you. Apply these energies well to your own refinement first. Your own full radiance will then gift your environment by simple resonance. Just your presence will affect your surroundings in a supportive and uplifting manner. This effect includes other individuals, for they will begin to resonate with you. Be gentle with these souls and call in my gifts to assist them, in maintaining their balance and firming their direction.

Changes are occurring now on Earth with increasing force and frequency. I offer my assistance in choosing and maintaining directions with balance. Breath deeply and call my name, Pralunizak, when life becomes overwhelming. Gentle is my touch, firm my directives. The choices are yours. With your request for my help, gladly do I assist you in managing and organizing these new energies into life supporting channels and activities. I am your chief operations officer, answering to you, the president. I am your support system, your gyroscope, to hold you on course. Lovingly I offer my services, and happily I perform them. I am Pralunizak, your Angel of Direction. ✿

Pralunizak
Angel of Direction

Anrisnoel

Angel of Tolerance

olerance is the acceptance of yourself and others where you and they are at the moment. Tolerance allows. All of you are on your way home, at different spots on the path, intentionally creating different experiences. Allow others their choices on how to live. Be tolerant of yourself for different needs and desires.

Everything is perfect in the moment and yet may change with different choices. No judgment. Allow. As your Angel of Tolerance, I bring you the energies to allow others their choice of creative ways to achieve their goals. As you learn and live tolerance, life becomes much simpler, with fewer tug of wars. Other's choices remain theirs, and you focus to see the value in their choices, even as you make your own choices.

Call me, Anrisnoel (*an rees' no el'*), your Angel of Tolerance, when activities and choices of yourself or others cause turmoil in your own life. Call me to help smooth your tender emotional triggers and to allow resolution of these old patterns into more supportive actions for all involved. Allow my help when family life and work become intolerable, when life develops sharp edges, when anger and bitterness bring a sour flavor to your mouth. Call me when more tolerance and understanding is needed, desired, or welcome.

Anris noel
Angel of Tolerance

Let me work my magic to soften your reactions to uncomfortable situations, and open your awareness to alternative choices, more creative actions. Call me and allow my energies to flex your rigid emotions into softened appreciation of another's efforts. Another's truth will be different from your own, for nature organizes to fulfill beliefs. As individuals you will have each grown into different beliefs so that different truths will *be truth* for others. Each person creates to the extent of his or her ability at any given moment. Appreciation of another's efforts only spurs them on to greater creations, love (with appreciation being a mild form of love) being a major ingredient in every phase. The viewer is indeed a cocreator along with the artist, sculptor, engineer, cook, wife, mother, father, gardener, et al.

Accept this role of tolerance to allow others their creative choices, for all need the freedom to progress homeward in their chosen way. Appreciation only fuels this homeward journey. I am Anrisnoel, your Angel of Tolerance, present and available to assist. I offer you blessings of tolerance. ✿

Esofael

Angel of Growth

rowth is the path of life. It is the result of letting go of the past, of creating new patterns of behavior, transitioning from situation to further directions and ideas, opening to new feelings and urges. Indeed growth includes changes on the physical, emotional, mental, and spiritual levels.

I am Esofael (*eh sof' ay el'*), your Angel of Growth, available now to assist you in all matters of growth. You are indeed enrolled in school house Earth, and *growth is the path and goals* along the way. It is the process of movement in life.

I offer my assistance in understanding and acknowledging this process, and in creating the steps through which you move. These steps lead to new doors and new awarenesses in life, as old beliefs and concepts are exchanged for more current truths and principles, tools to continue on the path of growth with ease and grace.

The process of life, with your budding desires, the guidance of Divine Will, trusting your own inner guidance as you make choices and accelerate through transitions, learning and completing lessons *is* the process of growth. Stagnation, holding on to the past, stifles growth and robs life of the divinely inspired flow of growth.

Open your mind to the flow of growth, with change as the only sure thing in life, the divine constant. Be in growth, fully embracing life's surging rhythms. Call me, Esofael, your Angel of Growth, when you want a companion along the way, or assistance in breaking through a particularly stubborn barrier in life. I open my heart and arms to assist you as you push forward in life, garnering the lessons learned and knowledge earned. I am Esofael, your Angel of Growth. ✿

Esofael
Angel of
Growth

Anrisielle

Angel of Light

E ver eager am I to share my brilliant gifts. I am Anrisielle (*ahn ree' see el*), your Angel of Light. My gift of Light energy, specifically balanced for humans, nebulous and glowing, will infuse your bodies with Light energy. You will feel lighter in weight, feel more light hearted, and look brighter as you merge my energies with yours.

All matter is just energy moving at different speeds or frequencies. My Light will assist in clearing blockages to your own Light's impeded flow, helping to prevent certain illnesses or to heal illnesses that have already begun to manifest obvious symptoms. My added Light energy can also assist in gently raising your Light levels. The result will be a pleasant sensation that you will most certainly desire to experience more often. Gradually you will be able to maintain more Light without my help.

The advantages of this are great. Many lessons will be more easily resolved, many unwanted and destructive tendencies more easily transmuted into constructive energies. More Light and higher frequencies gradually bring enlightenment and, generally speaking, an end to struggle. Invite my Light to assist in your darkness. Shed my Light on any and all problems to bring a quicker, more enlightened solution.

Anrisielle
Angel of Light

The entire human body is just energy, light at different densities and frequencies. My gift is to clarify this light, bring you from opaqueness to translucence, and increase your frequency, evidenced in increased brightness and clearer colors in your aura. These colors are also measures of frequencies. As you receive my gifts of Light, your radiance increases. You receive, and radiate this Light, sharing with your environment and other individuals, thus uplifting their values of Light.

All of life strives to increase Light value, this being seen as growth on the evolutionary scale. Open to my Light. This I freely offer to boost your energy, to enlighten your awareness, to soften your path. The more Light you accept, the more Light your systems can use. This Light is pure uplifting energy, a gift of God, transmuted to usable frequencies for you. Open to more Light, and you will become more of this Light. This is a *most* direct route to solving your 'problems' and lessons, for solutions are easily seen as your Light intensifies. Often lessons become transparent, and further steps a joy. I am your Angel of Light, Anrisielle, present at your call, to light your way and infuse your Being with Light. ✿

Larmeo

Angel of Universal Love

reetings and welcome to a world of Universal Love, a world of pure acceptance and appreciation for all you are and are becoming. I am Larmeo (*lar' me o'*), your Angel of Universal Love, here today to share the essence of my message for humanity and offer my assistance in creating this reality in your life now.

The joys of living in peace and harmony, in strength and joy are worth the journey through the morass of human growth and up the emotional ladder of life. I bring the energies of acceptance of all, understanding of the struggle of life, appreciation of each living the best way one knows. I bring universal acceptance of circumstance and choice, of each person's life and decisions therein.

The acceptance of others is a reflection of your personal acceptance within, a dawning of appreciation of yourself for a job well done, done as well as you could under the circumstances of life. I bring loving energies within and without, and through all of creation. This is recognition of yourself in others, of wholeness with creation, and Oneness with God.

This universal love is, therefore, totally personal, as you feel one with all others. It is also impersonal, for the feeling of Love for all, a universal, unconditional love, a love resplendent with allowance of all choices, is an aspect of this universal love. It is unconditional and total. How a person lives life is totally, unconditionally accepted as their choice.

My gift for humanity is this experience of universal love, complete with peace within and understanding, allowance, acceptance, and appreciation of all of creation. The experience of universal love is a life changing experience. This will cause an extensive resetting of internal behavior patterns, should you have any incongruent behaviors. Understanding, acceptance and appreciation of one's self far beyond any previous experience will occur quickly and easily as the joy of universal love becomes pervasively and expansively your experience. Life is then viewed through the angelic eyes of universal love for all of creation.

Join this party of joyous living in universal love. I am Larmeo, your Angel of Universal Love, at your service. ✿

Larmeo
Angel of
Universal
Love

Hillilael

Angel of Acceleration

ankind on Earth is now being energized with accelerating frequencies as the need for change and growth has become stringently evident. These higher frequency energies will assist all to move from inertia, or even a slow pace of change in life, to accelerated evolutionary changes.

These energies will feel increasingly uncomfortable if you choose to use them for other than opening your awareness to more Light and Love. This may mean recognizing and embracing a shadow within yourself and filling it with Light and Love.

Living in the past no longer serves. Live now, in the present, with an eye to the future, for this *now* is far different than any previous time. In a biblical sense it is the end times and, therefore, also the beginning time, the beginning of a new time for humanity with a different set of concepts, truths, and principles with which to live.

Know this to be true and act now from this moment. Open your mind and heart, and breathe in fully the essence of today. Even the dullest on Earth can feel the accelerating energies. Acknowledge that these energies are presented to assist you and access them fully and consciously, with forethought and intent to reconnect with God and be the cocreator of your moment.

Hillilaek

Angel of
Acceleration

At your request I, Hillilael (*hi' lee' lay el*), your Angel of Acceleration, can assist in opening your mind and heart to gracefully and easily grow in these times and energies. Many shadows, scars, hurts, and pains may surface as you turn your expectant face to the present and begin your personal acceleration. As you embrace these nurturing and generative energies, a wondrous new world will emerge within and without. I am on call now to assist as needed and desired. I am Hillilael. Just call! ✡

Naomaelle

Angel of Trust

am Naomaelle (*na o' ma el'*), your Angel of Trust, here to help open your heart and mind to your soul. You are One, heart, mind, and soul, yet often the heart or intellect operates independently of the whole. The more you dissociate within yourself, separating and rejecting parts of the Self, the less you trust. Your life and choices are then based on less and less information and knowingness as you segment the parts of yourself. Reconnection of these segmented parts leads to more knowingness, wholeness, and opens you to trust, trust in God, your Higher Self and the integrity of this wholeness, these connections of Oneness.

This reconnection within ultimately leads to trusting that God's divine plan of life for you is perfect. As you release your controls, your hanging on, and allow an unfolding *as you participate* in life, you and God create the ultimate for you. Trust. You are part of a divine team, and trust in your team will create far grander results than doing it alone. With trust re-established within your self, trust of others on Earth as part of your Earthly team becomes possible and enjoyable.

Often your creations in life, so full of hurt, pain, anger, and sorrow, seem foreign and opposite to the desired results. You feel failure, yet these creations often hold the core of a hard earned lesson on Earth, with stair step resolutions of chosen lessons in your earthly life. Trust allows a natural unfolding of your life lessons, an ease of movement which, should you staunch this flow with a lack of trust, may extend the lessons interminably and painfully.

Trust in God and participate in life. This is cocreation, not a solo act. Feel your feelings and move, divinely guided through life. Breathe deeply of each experience, fully present, trusting your connection with God and His divine guidance. Choose consciously and trust your knowingness, your God connection. Trust and breathe. Trust and move. Trust and live life fully.

I am your Angel of Trust, here to remind you of and assist you in reconnecting and trusting again. Trust and call me. I am Naomaelle, your Angel of Trust. ✿

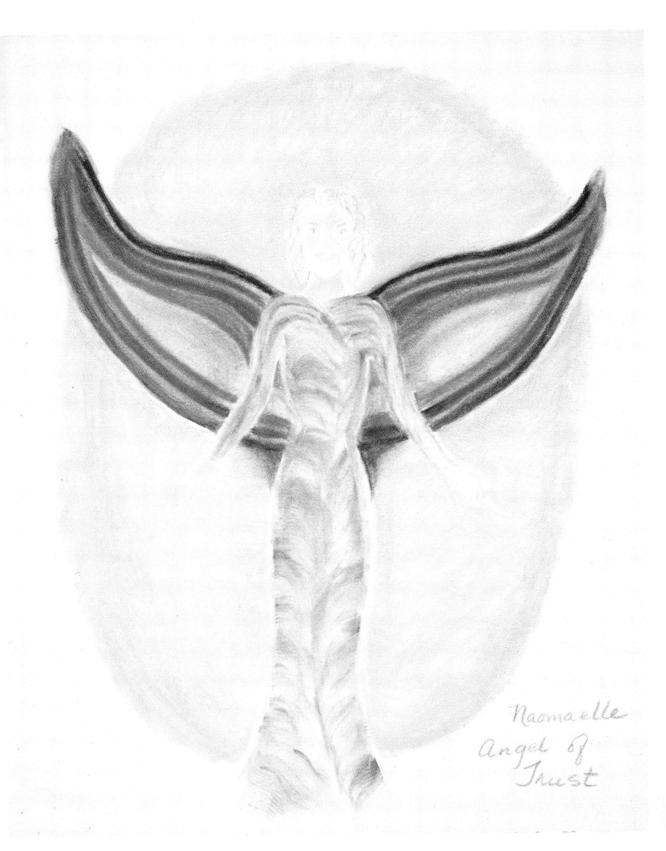

Naomaelle
Angel of
Trust

Anjeeliel

Angel of Sleep

I am Anjeeliel (*ahn jee' le el'*), your Angel of Sleep, here present to assist all who ask my assistance into the gentle conscious transition from waking state into sleep with awareness. Much of your lessons are completed and many higher frequency messages are received in sleep and in this transition period between wakefulness and sleep.

Awareness during sleep would be a great advantage. As you work with this awareness, it allows you to keep more and more memory of these sleep activities, thus pulling more and more higher frequency information into your third dimensional reality.

Allow my gentle ministrations as I help you hold awareness and even converse with you as you seep into sleep. Gradually your awareness and memories will open and become more meaningful. Sleep *can* be restful awareness instead of coma-like repose. As you come into greater balance, allowing and encouraging your bodies to heal, you will eagerly enter sleep state for the joy of this experience, instead of just the need of it.

I am Anjeeliel and gladly I will assist you in gaining balance and alignment, in opening to and hearing my guidance during rest. When possible, allow your body to remain in repose as you remain gently in sleep or semi-sleep awareness when

Anjeeliel
Angel of Sleep

beginning sleep or on waking. These moments of in-between time will acquaint you with the process of going back and forth over the threshold of wake and sleep, while gradually remaining in and gaining awareness.

Take me to bed with you! Let's play as you rest. A whole new world of awareness awaits you as you begin to work with me. Your nights will be full and busy, and yet you will awaken energized and excited about your day.

Try this. You'll like it, I promise. Take my hand as you go to bed, say my name, Anjeeliel, three times and close your eyes. In your mind call forth my essence and hold your desire for awareness during sleep, even for a moment, in gratitude and expectancy. From this moment forward we will be working and playing together during rest.

I can be helpful for those with unpleasant dreams, assisting you in resolution of issues causing these recurrent dreams. Insomniacs can also find benefit with me, for even insomniacs have gaps of restfulness where I can assist and gently resolve this condition. Sleep is a gold mine of joy and fun as your awareness opens to twenty-four hour a day consciousness. This *is* possible and advisable. You will find that as you gain more and more awareness during sleep, you will express more awareness during waking state as well. You will be a better candidate for working with all the other Angels.

Reclaim your alertness during sleep. I am Anjeeliel, your Angel of Sleep, present and ready to assist. Just call me. ✿

Elicenoel

The Angel of Beauty

J am your Angel of Beauty and I bring you the message that you are indeed a wondrous, beautiful creation of God. With the rays of truth and joy, I reflect the glory and perfection of creation back to you. Call on Me to assist in seeing the beauty of each moment on Earth, each situation, each encounter, and most of all, the beauty that you embody. You are a beauteous child of God, perfect and glorious in all aspects. My wings encircle you in the Love of God, only adding a soft and flowing border to the perfection incarnate.

I stand at your side awaiting your call, to see, feel, and be the beauty of creation. Let me assist in your creations of Love and Light, as I add my Angelic Essence to your creative energies. Call on me at any time, and especially when help is needed in seeing the beauty and perfection of the moment.

I am your loving servant in the Light. I am Elicenoel (*e lees' no el'*) and I carry the beauty of the Angels to you. I bring you, my wondrous child of beauty, the beauty of universes to be seen and felt in this moment. My web of magic spans dimensions as I reach out and embrace your soul to enliven your awareness of your own beauty and the joyous beauty of all creation.

Feel the connection, my embrace to you, and your connection to all around you. Expand into the magic of the beauty and perfection in and around you. Beauty becomes more apparent as I stretch my web of influence, connecting across dimensions to include your own, alerting you to your Beingness, your true Self, divine in its own right. My dance spans the rainbow of colors of your dimension, and much more.

Call on me for assistance in creating beauty on all levels. Become the conscious cocreator of beauty with me as your partner. I reflect your beauty back to you, oh wondrous child of beauty and light. Feel my embrace and ever request my help as I stand ready and eager to lend a hand. I am Elicenoel, your Angel of Beauty. ✡

Elicenoel
Angel of Beauty

Menowrael

Angel of Transition

A s all of Earth goes through changes at this time, my assistance helps to actuate those changes. My boost now will energize your choices to actualities. I, Menowrael (*me now' ra el'*), come at the fullness of completions, ready for change and renewed growth, transitioning into the fullness of Being within the Self. I offer excellent assistance for those of you poised to make changes within, with locations, with work and home life, in any and all areas of life.

Open your hearts, breathe through all the blocks in your bodies, feeling my assistance flow to you now, with your permission, as you choose and move to create. I will assist in all your changes, with special attention to great, far reaching changes.

A transition point can be likened to an area where water meets land. This change-over point draws the attention strongly to successfully maneuver the changing terrain. A more gentle change would be meadow to woods. It still draws clear attention to maneuver. Switch points in life are like this, and recognition of one of these, with the requisite attention to new situations needing new ways of handling and living, will make life more of an adventure than a drudgery.

Menowrael
Angel of Transition

These switch points may mean you have completed a portion of your commitment and mission, with new doors opening to welcome you. Graciously walk through these into your new life. Switch points can also happen within a mission, to change a direction or way of achieving a desired result. These accelerating energies introduce new knowledge and shed new light on a situation, for a quicker, more enlightened outcome. This can be accessed or refused by choice.

Free will versus determinism comes into play. If change is refused, crises mount as repetitive choices are presented, with increasing intensity, God's and your way of pushing you to resolution and openness to growth. Change is the only constant in life. Use these energies, wisely accessing them. Ride the wave of acceleration, applying these energies to desired growth, breathing deeply of God's Love and Light, appreciating the push of life as the pull of God back to His arms, with a harvest of Love our gifts to Him.

I am Menowrael, your Angel of Transition, at your service. Call on me for ease and grace in transition, with love and appreciation for the gift of energies for change. Please call me at your need. ✿